LITERACY
MOVES
OUTDOORS

VALERIE BANG-JENSEN

LITERACY MOVES OUTDOORS

Learning Approaches
for Any Environment

Heinemann · Portsmouth, NH

Heinemann
145 Maplewood Avenue, Suite 300
Portsmouth, NH 03801
www.heinemann.com

> *Heinemann's authors have devoted their entire careers to developing the unique content in their works, and their written expression is protected by copyright law. We respectfully ask that you do not adapt, reuse, or copy anything on third-party (whether for-profit or not-for-profit) lesson-sharing websites.*
>
> **—Heinemann Publishers**

"Dedicated to Teachers" is a trademark of Greenwood Publishing Group, LLC.

The author and publisher wish to thank those who have generously given permission to reprint borrowed material:

Figs. 1–1, 3–7: © Haile Hamlett / Figs. 2–2, 7–8: © Abigail Bernier / Fig. 2–5: © Faith Horton / Figs. 2–6, 2–19, 4–3: © Patrick Bohan / Fig. 2–7: © Stannard Baker / Fig. 2–8: © Jon Hyde & Kimberly Sultze / Figs. 2–16 to 2–18, 5–3j: © Cat Wright Parrish / Fig. 3–8: © Maura D'Amore / Fig. 3–13: © Aziza Malik; nature images: © Kayla Chaplin / Fig. 4–10: © Diana Geller / Figs. 4–17 to 4–19: © Drena Varghese / Fig. 4–21: © Brian MacDonald Photography / Fig. 5–3: © Coastal Maine Botanical Gardens; ladybug: © Alekss/Adobe Stock/HIP; daisy: © PhotoLink/Photodisc/Getty Images/HIP; potatoes: © Silkstock/Adobe Stock / Figs. 5–3g, 5–11, 6–12: © Morris Arboretum, University of Pennsylvania / Figs. 5–9, 5–10: © Aziza Malik / Figs. 6–8 to 6–10: © Swim Pony Performing Arts, Bri Barton and Meg Lemieur / Fig. 5–10: slide image © Aziza Malik; animal images © Joe Resteghini

Library of Congress Control Number: 2023930868
ISBN: 978-0-325-13754-4

Editor: Zoë Ryder White
Production: Vicki Kasabian
Cover and text designs: Vita Lane
Typesetting: Kim Arney
Manufacturing: Val Cooper

Printed in the United States of America on acid-free paper
1 2 3 4 5 VP 28 27 26 25 24 23   PO 4500868528

For Eleanor,
Henry, and Orla,
who love reading the outdoors

CONTENTS

Acknowledgments   ix

1 Move Literacy Outdoors 1

Why Move Literacy Outdoors?   2

What Will You Find in This Book?   6

Try One Thing   7

2 Literacy to Go 9

Seize the Opportunity: Prepare for Spontaneity!   9

Ready? Scaling Up from (Almost) Zero Preparation to Mindful Planning   16

Resources   32

3 StoryWalks® 33

What Is a StoryWalk®?   33

Logistics: How to Make a StoryWalk®   39

From Reading StoryWalks® to Writing Them: Helping Students Create Their Own Story Experiences   41

Resources   48

4 Word Gardens 50

What Is a Word Garden?   50

The Power of a Word Garden   51

Logistics: How to Make a Word Garden   51

Curricular Explorations in a Word Garden   56

Last Words   65

Resources   67

5 Show Us a Sign! 69

Students Use Signs to Solve Problems and Interpret Their World

Why Study Signage?	69
Interpretive Signage	79
Resources	89

6 Literacy Trails 90

Trails Take Us Somewhere New	90
Which Path to Take?	91
Resources	107

7 Make It Happen 108

Strategies and Resources to Help You Move Literacy Outdoors

Inspired and Ready to Get Started?	108
Resources	117

Children's Books Cited	119
Professional Works Cited	130

Acknowledgments

My editor Zoë Ryder White once observed that my colorful Post-it Note outline for a new chapter reminded her of one of my quilts. In fact, writing a book is a lot like making a quilt, and I have pieced this one together with ideas, questions, and resources generously offered by friends, teachers, students, experts in many areas, and of course, kids.

Editors are heroes, too often unsung. I owe many thanks to Katie Wood Ray for shaping me up in my first Heinemann book, tweaking the title for this one, and especially for arranging an editorial blind date with Zoë Ryder White . . . thank you, Zoë, for swiping right. In a book about literacy and the outdoors, I so appreciated the poet in you and your gracious way with words. Your feedback—direct and often tinged with humor—always moved my ideas in a better direction. Your quilt square would, of course, feature a ditch embroidered with *lost words*.

The binding of this quilt is surely threaded by Heinemann. As a clear advocate for and champion of teachers in a climate that is increasingly challenging, Heinemann supports innovative and student-centered teaching and learning. Thank you for the opportunity to contribute to this work.

A large crew has contributed to this project. I am amazed and humbled by the design and production work by Vita Lane and Vicki Kasabian that makes the book more appealing than I had even hoped or imagined. Sonja Chapman and Catrina Swasey stepped in to make the process as seamless as possible. Elizabeth Silvis, thank you for your enthusiasm for this project and for connecting readers with this book.

Many quilt contributions came from a broadly based school crew, including teachers, an administrative assistant extraordinaire, and a principal who creates his own StoryWalks®! Hilary Hamilton, Aziza Malik, Haile Hamlett, Kayla Chaplin, Betsy Patrick, Joe Resteghini, and Janet Breen—thank you. SMC alums Meghan Feenan, Kristin Funsten, Faith Horton, Elyse Gentile, Callie Goss, Michelle Jacobs, Abbie Bernier, Hanna Lesch, Matt Hajdun, and all of you Zoom focus group participants are represented—of course—by purple and gold squares.

Experts like Melissa Stewart, Shelly Waterman, Adrienne Mackey, Amy Ludwig VanDerwater, Zoe Richards, Ben Rodgers, Maja Smith, Sandra Murphy, and Jim Brangan were generous with their time and patiently answered my questions. I learned so much from all of you and hope that you can recognize some of your wisdom in these pages.

Artists' work inspired and improved the messages in the book. Patrick Bohan and John Hyde—teachers will appreciate the clarity of your contributions in the form of sharp photographs in the Montana snow and of homemade wooden word "stones." Chris and Kim Cleary, of On the Rocks Carving Studio in Jericho, Vermont—your square would feature the initial "word salad" that has launched word gardens around the world. Your beautiful stones grace many of the pages of this book.

And the kids! Kids at Champlain, Cambridge, and Underhill ID schools, plus Rufus and Frank D'Amore, Jill Knight, and Will and Reed Haslam and their families filled this book with unique ideas and voice.

Saint Michael's College might serve as the quilt batting: invisible to the eye but infusing the project with warmth. The support of the Teaching Gardens, and subsequent Word Garden and StoryWalks®, is the genesis of this book, along with the opportunity of a sabbatical to bring it to fruition. I especially appreciate how my departmental colleagues rallied during a challenging year to make it work for me. Amy Knight introduced me to just the right experts in her circle and Rebecca Haslam picked up many of the pieces my absence left.

Librarians rock. Kristen Hindes, Anthony Bassignani, Stacey Knight, and the whole crew at Durick Library provided interlibrary loan, due-date extensions, tech help, and an always-welcoming front desk. Megan Estey Butterfield, children's librarian at Fletcher Free Library, provided the backstory for STEAM kits and StoryWalks®; I'm so glad to learn about the role that public libraries can play in a pandemic!

Although quilting bees were not an option during the pandemic, friends still offered support, ideas, and advice. Thank you to Olivia and Peter Rukavina for hosting a global Zoom conversation that helped me launch this project early in the process. Alison Blay-Palmer and Maura D'Amore's squares would feature the colors found on beach and farm walks where they generously listened as I worked through ideas. Diane Anderson, I loved sharing our sabbaticals and look forward to the completion of your project. Somehow Mary Beth Doyle managed to send me timely texts of support just when I needed them. Kristen Hindes seamlessly merged her friend role with super reference librarian help; surely her square would have a Z for Zotero.

My dear friend, colleague, and frequent coauthor, Mark Lubkowitz, offered up direct and caring advice—mostly on his drive home. Writing was not quite as much fun without you and I definitely ate less chocolate. Ready to write the next book?

My sister, daughters, and their families, Judith, Bree, Travis, Nell, Justin, Eleanor, Henry, and Orla, would have the squares representing patience, interest, and enthusiasm. From Amherst to Philadelphia, Seattle, and Prince Edward Island, you supported me by scouting out local book experiences, arboretums, and signage. Thank you for waiting while I took *just one more photo*, for celebrating the book contract, and for cheering me on in general.

And for my husband, Lars, a square smack in the middle of this book quilt, edged with hearts. Your unwavering belief in this project powered me through the newer and rougher ideas. Thank you for the walks and talks, and the constant willingness to help me think something through. Your comments and questions improved every aspect of this project.

MOVE LITERACY OUTDOORS

Haile's first graders bundle into their snowsuits and boots, ready for the grand opening of their ABC StoryWalk®. Each student has written a page based on what was growing in the school garden in the fall, prompted by a photograph. Ivy looks for her contribution, *T Is for Trowel*, and Ray for his: *D Is for Dirt*. The class walks from post to post, chanting the words aloud, and during the course of this literacy-based walk they practice alphabetic order, revisit garden curriculum content, and enjoy being outside. Haile has created an outdoor literacy experience that invites her students to consider purpose, audience, and discovery. And she is confident that they will also begin to see that they can take their emerging literacy skills wherever they go.

If you're wondering what literacy might look like outside the classroom, it's everywhere. The first word a young child may learn to read is STOP, a useful directive encountered at crosswalks and streets everywhere. Supermarkets use signage to direct us to items on our shopping lists, and once we find them other signs identify the product and price. At the local museum,

Figure 1-1

a docent engages a gathered group with snippets of history stories bulleted on her clipboard. We may encounter poetry chalked on sidewalks or stapled among advertisements on the bulletin board of a local convenience store. Pages of a gorgeous picture book are posted to entice hikers on a story walk up a hill through the woods, alerting them along the path to the way that different birds build their nests. Literacy can be everywhere; like Haile's students, reading and writing outside the classroom enables us to appreciate and connect to our broader community and world. These experiences also offer young writers power and agency in considering audience for literacy in authentic settings.

Why Move Literacy Outdoors?

If there has been a silver lining of any kind to the pandemic, it's that social distancing compelled many teachers to think nimbly, and this meant that when they could, they moved their classes outdoors. A tough challenge at first, but once new routines were established and curricular adaptations made—think sensory paths, nature journals, and phonics treasure hunts—teachers discovered unanticipated benefits. During a recent focus group discussion, anecdotes poured in. Third-grade teacher Abbie noticed that everyone is calm and more settled back in the classroom after being outside for a lesson. Special educator Kristin observed that her students are better able to focus on learning when she balances outdoor and indoor experiences. And Caitlin, an upper-elementary science teacher, described how twice-weekly nature journal writing has been transformative for her students; their ability to make specific observations is transferring into all of their writing.

Outdoors is the new classroom

My thinking about literacy outdoors pays homage to powerful thinking about outdoor learning, learning about nature, and ways of being outside with children. Recent leaders in the field, like Richard

Figure 1-2   All you need for outdoor journaling is a notebook and pencil.

Louv, David Sobel, Juliet Robertson, Herb Broda, and others, have provided compelling arguments about the value of getting children outside. Louv (2008, 7) writes that nature demands ". . . the full use of the senses." Being outdoors invites us to notice in new ways, to be affected by sound, smell, and tactile experiences that are part of our world yet are different from those available indoors. Juliet Robertson (2014, 2) observes that "outdoor learning is an umbrella term which covers every type of learning experience which happens outdoors," including playground games, environmental education, and "adventurous activities." She notes that being outdoors is a key part of physical development, requiring navigation of territory and problem-solving. Much of the current focus is on nature-based education, and the proliferation of Forest Kindergartens, outdoor classrooms, nature centers, and nature-oriented summer programs reflects this. In his accessible and thorough book, *Schoolyard-Enhanced Learning: Using the Outdoors as an Instructional Tool, K–8*, Broda (2007, 20) notes that "language arts concepts seem more immediate and compelling when you are trying to share what you have experienced in the environment." You will find that many of the ideas in this book lean

Outdoors Is for Every Learner

Just as you do in creating any part of your curriculum, you'll be thinking about your individual learners and their needs, past experiences, and ways of moving through the world as you plan for outdoor learning. You'll want to anticipate how you can help each student find their *way into* what you have planned for outdoors. Some students need clear and direct boundaries and directions; others might need help physically navigating outdoor spaces. Anticipating and planning will set up all your students for success. Invite school support teams, families, and the students themselves to offer advice. Among other considerations, you will want to think about:

- Surfaces for students using crutches, wheelchairs, or walkers: gravel, dirt, wood, grass, concrete, and asphalt bring their own strengths and challenges.

- Choices for how to participate: How many different movements could a spiral symbol inspire? Could it be spinning on one's feet? Twirling oneself or being spun in a wheelchair? Brainstorming possibilities with your class will broaden their interpretations.

- Approaches to safety: Will students need partners? What are the boundaries? How will students express their needs?

- Multimodal directions: What will your students need to understand what to do on the trail? Using a combination of symbols, words, and a combination of audio and visual directions will support your learners.

- Clear routines and boundaries: these are explored explicitly in Chapter 2.

And, just like teaching in any area, observing how things go and checking in with your students will allow for subsequent thoughtful revision of your strategies and approaches that will help you and your students have increasingly successful experiences outdoors.

Figure 1-3 Words and symbols together create a complete message.

heavily on nature-oriented outdoor learning, but this is not my focus. This book invites you specifically and enthusiastically to move literacy outdoors wherever you are.

Finding ways into outdoor literacy learning

For many students, *literacy* means the reading and writing they do in the classroom, yet reading and writing happen everywhere we go. Purpose, audience, and place are compelling reasons to shape writing and reading when literacy moves out of the classroom and into real world settings, both natural and engineered. Your school setting will shape the ways that you might implement the approaches in this book, and I have made suggestions along the way for rural, suburban, and urban schools. You will also find some beginning guidelines related to *universal design*. These include efforts to make learning experiences accessible to all students, enabling them to be independent and participate in a variety of ways. You'll want to consider space, safety, and strategies to support a wide range of literacy and language skills. Specific and expanded guidelines, plus *7 principles* may be found on the website for the Centre for Excellence in Universal Design.

Ways in for varied settings

There are multiple ways to create experiences outside the classroom that invite students to make discoveries about literacy, particularly about purpose and audience. I've provided a continuum for different levels of investment in terms of your time and materials. You might

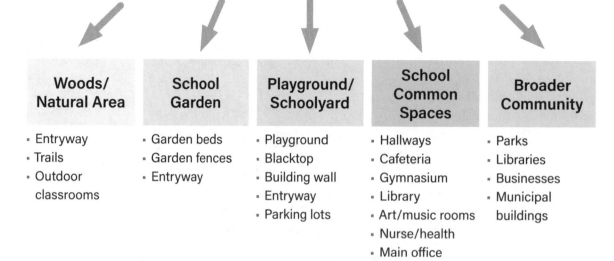

Figure 1-4   Find your starting place for moving literacy outside the classroom.

be ready to dip your toe into literacy outdoors on a beautiful day with the "literacy to go" backpacks. If you're ready to reshape a whole curricular unit on writing to inform, the chapter on signage might work for you as your starting point. A StoryWalk® might be the perfect way to have a celebration of your poetry unit. Find your way in and move on from there!

Essential terms for moving literacy outdoors

For the purposes of this book, *literacy* means being able to draw, read, or write for one's own purposes and a specific audience. Haile's first graders drew their alphabet pages to display their understanding of the alphabet and to inform the school community about the garden. Additionally, to *be literate* in a particular setting means that you have the knowledge you need to serve your purpose. For example, being *garden literate* might mean that you recognize when plants need water or more sunlight. Being *school literate* might mean that you know to go to the nurse if you scrape your knee or to the library when you need a book. Being literate about the outdoors in your setting might include knowing about safety, the weather, and boundaries.

In defining *outdoors*, I have tried to include many settings, from blacktop play yards to neighborhoods and schools lucky enough to have a small patch of woods. Because there may be school situations where it is not possible for students to go outdoors, I have made suggestions about adapting some of the approaches in this book to indoor hallways and communal spaces like libraries, gyms, and cafeterias. It is my hope that as a society we will find ways to get all children outdoors. Outdoors in your setting beyond your school might include neighborhood sidewalks, playgrounds and fields, parks, gardens, green spaces, and downtowns.

Forming partnerships in the broader school community and beyond

Moving literacy outside the classroom opens up collaborations with teacher specialists in areas such as art, music, and physical education, as well as librarians, administrators, and other staff. For example, StoryWalks® invite students to consider which pieces they write—or books they read— might contribute to the purpose of a nurse's office, the cafeteria, or library. One music teacher created a "song walk" using stanzas of a favorite song placed throughout the playground. An art teacher developed a unit on shape; posting pages of a Lois Ehlert book could help the school community see

Bringing the Outside In

One clear lesson learned from the recent pandemic is flexibility. Hopefully, our unpredictable moments will be caused by more mundane and seasonal events such as weather as we move forward, but there may be times when switching up to digital or virtual experiences makes the most sense. Firsthand and hands-on experiences allow students to experience and learn in the most immediate way, but resources such as videos and apps may be tapped to help bring the outside in. While "virtual outdoors" may seem like a contrast in ideas, teachers are finding ways to connect the two. Podcasts, QR codes, and videos offer possible modes for sharing the outdoors with both in-person and virtual audiences. After studying these digital modes of sharing and publishing, students could create their own.

how Ehlert uses the elements of shape and color to convey animals and flowers. Community partnerships might be formed around a civic effort such as transportation or urban green spaces. *Last Stop on Market Street* could be posted at bus stops; books from the One Small Square nature series (Silver and Wynne 1995) or *Nature in the Neighborhood* (Morrison 2004) could invite sidewalk observations.

What Will You Find in This Book?

You will find five broad approaches to literacy that you can move outdoors: *Literacy to Go*, *Word Gardens*, *StoryWalks®*, *Interpretive Signage*, and *Literacy Trails*. Each has its own chapter, and I have offered first steps, varied entry points, logistics, literacy connections, and ways that you can level up once you're ready. All these approaches incorporate excellent children's books—relevant beginning lists of both fiction and nonfiction titles are offered, and I am sure you'll add some of your favorites as you try things out.

The various approaches offer a chance to experience different aspects of literacy, but you will find some common elements. All of them use visual literacy to communicate meaning, and encourage student writers to consider audience needs and the relationship of the text to the setting. And each approach invites you to discover platforms for literacy learning that are authentic to specific settings, and offers resources for launching projects.

Chapter 2: Literacy to Go

When the opportunity arises, seize the moment to move literacy outside. Here you'll find suggestions for developing literacy backpacks and kits full of books, guides, and writing implements based on themes like *trees*, *architecture*, and *birds*. This chapter provides a first step for teachers who are new to literacy outdoors, short on time, or need a quick start for any reason. Suggestions are offered for a range of outdoor literacy experiences from read-alouds to phonics. Guidelines for gathering materials, determining routines, and setting the foundation for behavior outdoors are offered. Models will be provided for teachers and students eager to create their own *grab-and-go* opportunities.

Chapter 3: StoryWalks®

StoryWalks® describes a popular practice that invites readers to combine a reading experience with a walk, often providing the opportunity for connecting text with place. You'll find guidelines on how to choose books, set up the walk, and involve your students in writing their own texts for a story experience. Publishing their own writing for a walk experience provides an authentic reason for students to consider audience, topic, and editing.

Chapter 4: Word Gardens

Word Gardens are a lot like magnetic poetry, only bigger so that they are accessible to a whole class and invite movement and wordplay. This chapter shares different ways that schools have created words by etching or painting stones or pieces of wood. Explore the ways that you can incorporate word gardens into areas of your curriculum; examples include word study, poetry, social studies, science, and guidance.

Chapter 5: Show Us a Sign! Students Use Signs to Solve Problems and Interpret Their World

Signs solve problems. Effective signs, whether for a grocery store, library, or nature trail, require knowing the purpose, audience, type of language, and options for images to convey the message to a viewer. This chapter provides teachers with a model, criteria for different types of signage, and strategies for supporting students in solving the challenges of informing and directing readers in many contexts. Examples include school signage and garden signage, as well as creating signage for curricular celebrations or installations of outdoor learning.

Chapter 6: Literacy Trails

You'll learn about ways to create trails that help your students practice and apply skills and concepts, as well as develop other trails that help them explore natural settings. Building on the interpretive signage explored in Chapter 5, trails may be a perfect way for your students to share what they are learning in history or social studies. Many cities are developing urban trails or walks. Developing your own can be an authentic way to create curriculum relating to visual text, such as symbols, maps, photographs, and interpretive signage to explore community highlights. What might this look like in your urban, suburban, or rural community?

Chapter 7: Make It Happen: Strategies and Resources to Help You Move Literacy Outdoors

Looking for clear and direct tips for administrative support, finding funding, and potential community partners? Here's where you'll find them, along with suggestions for creating space and finding like-minded colleagues to move literacy outdoors. Favorite resources are provided for those who want to dig deeper into nature-oriented learning.

Try One Thing

By the end of the book, you'll be ready to set up poetry walks, paint stones with word families, and create interpretive signage for the school-wide open house. Sitting in on a second-grade professional learning community team meeting recently, I heard one teacher gently encourage colleagues to *just try one thing.* She was acknowledging the exhaustion that many of her peers were feeling and wanted them to take one small step to get their students outdoors. She urged, "We don't need to worry about a budget—the reality is that kids are content sitting on simple towels, yoga mats, stumps—a clipboard is all you need!" Like Haile and the first-grade

ABC walk, this teacher knew that literacy outdoors is motivating and can provide authentic purposes for student readers and writers.

We can use literacy to weave learning together and to build strong school communities. While classrooms are separate and discrete spaces, the outdoors belongs to everyone—a shared space for everyone in the whole school to explore and gather. Outdoor learning initiatives can lead to shared inquiries, problem-solving, and celebration, supporting literacy learning all the while. Pick a chapter and *try one thing*.

2

LITERACY TO GO

Seize the Opportunity: Prepare for Spontaneity!

It's the first sunny day after a drab few weeks and everyone wants to get outside. You grab your current read-aloud—novel or picture book—and head outside with your class. The students settle in, eager to hear the next chapter, and you all enjoy the change of setting. You've just moved literacy outside in a spontaneous moment. In this chapter, you'll find ways to get outside with your class on the spur of the moment with almost no planning, to other ways that will be easy to launch once you've done some preparation for materials and routines ahead of time. Somewhat surprisingly, the secret to spontaneity is planning! I am more likely to get in my daily walk when I know where my sneakers are, have my step counter strapped to my wrist, my podcasts queued up, and my water bottle filled. With everything in place, it's easy to seize the moment and get outdoors, and to be honest, I'm more likely to do it. The same idea is true in an artist's studio and a biologist's lab. When materials are set up, whether it be the microscope, sterilized petri dishes, and specimens, or paint palette, brushes, canvas, and lighting, when everything is always ready, we can move seamlessly into the work at hand.

Planning for literacy outdoors will enable you to be spontaneous when the weather cooperates or opportunities arise. The rain has stopped? The art teacher has gone home sick?

Schedules change at the last minute on a regular basis for a variety of reasons. With all the materials ready and logistics taken care of ahead of time you'll be ready to seize the moment.

Structures, routines, and materials

Remember how you prepare to work with your class at the beginning of the school year for the ways you will come together and function as a learning community? To move literacy outside, you'll want to establish some predictable routines and expectations. For some students, being outside during school may be a new experience, and whether they ask explicitly or not, you'll need to anticipate questions like: *What will I need to take when we go out? Where do we meet? How do we work together?* Discussion, modeling, and self-critique will help them internalize your guidelines or rules for working outside and develop competence and independence. As part of a school/city partnership, Ben Rodgers, a Conservation Field Officer with the local parks and recreation department, works with students outdoors on various projects. He wants students to internalize ways of working together and creating relationships that they take everywhere—inside, outside, in their homes, and in their communities. Since district school norms are *Be Safe, Be Respectful, and Be Responsible,* he sees those as the touchstones for working together outdoors, too. While these norms are similar to the ones that help everyone function inside the school, Faith Horton, a third-grade teacher who takes her class outside regularly, cautions her students that *we are creating a space where we behave and experience in a specific way that may be somewhat different from inside.* Together with your students, you might make anchor charts like the one in Figure 2–1 listing student ideas about ways of working together outside, emerging from class discussions. You might even print them out and ask students to tape these to their nature journals on the inside cover. Talk through very practically about what will happen if there is a fire drill, or a student needs to use the bathroom or go to the nurse. Like any other predictable part of their school experience, familiar routines and materials help students approach outdoor experiences as part of their regular learning. Be sure to note and discuss successes with your class and colleagues as well as figure out how to smooth out any bumps. Just as we know it takes the first month or so of school to establish routines inside our classrooms, it will take some repeated visits outside to establish this new setting as a place for learning and exploration.

Space

Outdoor spaces at schools vary considerably. For some, finding a place on the blacktop that's off the beaten recess path will be the goal, for others, a nearby park or grassy area on the playground may be an option. Teachers in suburban and rural schools may have outdoor bounty and create designated learning spaces. At one rural school the community donated tree stumps to the playground and students shaped and fired clay animal plaques that were then attached to the stumps (see Figure 2–2). Each student had a specific stump for outdoor sessions, and the area quickly became an outdoor classroom. Benches of any type—camping seats or chairs, yoga mats, or foam pads—can all help create a learning space and give students an anchor as they learn the ropes of an outdoor classroom.

Figure 2-1 Class-generated norms organized into: Be Safe, Be Respectful, and Be Prepared.

Other outdoor elements can support literacy; the high school technology center in one district built little libraries for each of the schools. If you can find a book outside, you can read it outside! Little libraries (Figure 2–3) provide easy access to a changing collection of books; families and community members may donate books and feel that they are contributing to literacy efforts. Students love donating reproductions of their own work, whether laminated poems or copies of their writing in book form. One teacher created an opportunity for curated feedback to student authors using a QR code and a message: *Did you enjoy this book? The author would love to hear from you. Please send your comments using this QR code.* Procedures for sharing student work this way will ensure it's not a one-off event, but part of the regular options for publishing student writing.

Time

Time is our currency in schools, and we rarely have enough. Ultimately, in the eyes of our students, what we spend our time on is what we value. If we make time to get outside, from

Figure 2–2

the quick read-aloud or walk to a longer, more deliberate experience, our students will view themselves as readers and writers everywhere. They will also discover new topics, types of text, and purposes for literacy.

The transition from inside to outside and back can be a deterrent for teachers because of the time required to help get everyone ready. One teacher grabs her read-aloud book and then meets her class outside after physical education for an outdoor read. Another takes them outside before their lunch recess. Both approaches limit the time spent in travel and even finding jackets.

It may make sense and be manageable to aim for once a week.

Figure 2–3

What Day Is It?

One way to go is to give each day of the week a nickname that suggests an outdoor activity. Students enjoy anticipation and predictability, and this can be one way to create a planning routine for yourself and colleagues. Surely your students will have some great suggestions, too!

Monday	*Mindful Mondays* might involve yoga outside or spending time in *sit spots*, observing. If you've got a mountain nearby, you're set with *Mountain Mondays*.
Tuesday	*Tuneful Tuesdays* could be for singing together outside; if you've got willing music teachers, bring them along. *Take Out Tuesday* would suggest taking books outside. *Treasure Hunt Tuesdays* could be just the day for scavenger hunts.
Wednesday	*Wednesdays* might be *wild*, or invite *wonder*, or involve *walks*. Reading Caldecott Honor Book *Wonder Walkers* (Archer 2021) would be a great touchstone as it encourages wild wondering about the outdoors.
Thursday	An easy catch-all here is *Thinking Thursdays*, but as we want students to be thinking every day, you might want to feature *Talk and Walk Thursdays*. *Treasure Hunt Thursday* or *Take Out Thursday* work just as well alliteratively as they do with Tuesday.
Friday	Fridays might be for *frolicking* or *finding* things, whether you have access to a *forest* or not.

Figure 2–4

Some lucky schools have dedicated days of the week to specific outdoor experiences. One rural school experimented with Forest Fridays, with a designated time for each class to spend in the woods; their success and location led to the addition of their Mountain Mondays. At another school, with an extra twenty minutes in his Wednesday schedule, one teacher has instituted what he calls *Wednesday Walk and Snack* where his fifth graders bring their snacks and walk with a buddy. A simple prompt about a favorite book or a prediction could deepen the talk; you might think about setting up these walking partnerships with the care that you would for any *turn and talk* pairings.

Materials

Students may need the same literacy tools for their work outside as they use inside. Each student might have a tub, bin, tote, backpack, seating mat, chalk, clipboard, writing implement,

Figure 2-5   During the pandemic, one school created "to go" bins for outdoor learning. They've been so successful that they plan to continue this practice. Each bin and item share a number, so restocking them is easy if an item goes astray.

Figure 2-6   Hand-held plastic magnifying glasses work well for explorers to examine things up close.

If You're Doing It Inside, You Can Do It Outside

Two teachers describe how they see indoor literacy as outdoor literacy. Primary-grade teacher Michelle Jacobs works at a school with a structured, nonnegotiable phonics curriculum. She doesn't miss a beat in moving this work outside. Michelle uses twigs or chalk with her students to make Elkonin or sound boxes for work in segmenting sounds in words. She sends them off to find "something with a short a vowel sound," or "something that starts with a /b/ sound." When she taught in an urban Illinois school, she found that chalked hopscotch templates were a great way to practice different types of word work. Students are given a word from a current phonic pattern to create a hopscotch using one box for each sound and hop through each other's boxes, tapping out and blending words as they go; this would be an active way to practice sight words, too. Michelle finds ways to use natural objects to help students develop phonemic awareness.

Students might gather pebbles, acorns, or leaves, and draw three boxes for consonant/vowel/consonant words. Michelle asks them to place a pebble in the box that represents the beginning, middle, or end sound. Her students love the scavenger hunts she designs to help them practice word/sound knowledge. Once she knows which objects are available outside, she asks them to:

- Find something that begins with a given sound.
- Find something that rhymes with _____.

Students each bring a found object to the meeting spot, and then she invites the class as a whole to name three words that rhyme with each found object.

Michelle's students build letters using natural objects such as leaves, grass, sticks, or stones. Students could write their own words, or the teacher might dictate a currently relevant word based on a word pattern. Students could also meet this challenge using sidewalk chalk, drawing in sand, or snow.

Figure 2-7

Figure 2-8

Callie Goss, a fifth-/sixth-grade Language Arts teacher, describes a poetry unit based on the *Doors of Poetry* created by Georgia Heard. Callie finds that students are inspired by the outdoors when writing poetry through the lenses of the *Wonder Door*—things they are wondering about or questions they have, and the *Observation Door*—things they observe in the world around them. Moving online, Callie's students are fascinated by Twitter thread stories—short episodic fiction or nonfiction narratives spun out over numerous tweets. One student launched a thread story using the school's outdoor story boards, enticing readers along by posting hard copies of the tweets that told her story.

Michelle and Callie have made it a practice to think about how their *inside literacy* might look as *outside literacy*. Scottish outdoor educator Juliet Robertson (2014, 1) notes that we have been "conditioned" to think "indoors" when it comes to teaching. When we move literacy practices outside we give students the message that reading, writing, and thinking go with them no matter where they are.

pencil, and crayons. One third-grade teacher claims that a pencil sharpener can make or break a session outside if you're expecting students to write! A class set of good quality plastic hand lenses is relatively inexpensive and will allow for close examination of all sorts of objects, textures, and tiny things. Several teachers remarked that old towels and yoga mats were lifesavers when moving class outside during the pandemic.

Ready? Scaling Up from (Almost) Zero Preparation to Mindful Planning

Think about moving literacy outdoors as a continuum; you can dip your toe in, wade in up to your knees, or plunge in, depending on your setting, students, curriculum, and interest. There are lots of reasons to get your students outside, from a simple change of pace to the development of an appreciation for the outdoors, no matter where you are. Reading and writing are tools for learning about new environments, and outdoor settings offer the chance for your readers to use their senses to observe and experience elements not typically encountered indoors.

Start by grabbing a book

Grabbing a book and going outside requires little to no preparation. One fifth-grade teacher in New England confided to me that the first sunny spring day after a long cold winter is all she needs to grab the current read-aloud and head outside. Diving into a chapter or two of a familiar book means that students already know the characters and setting, and you can get right to it. Cold ground? Savvy teachers include an old towel or yoga mat on their class supply list or stockpile these to share with their classes. Listening to a favorite book together outside builds a communal sense of literacy and offers the message that reading is a great activity for outdoors. If you have independent reading time on your schedule, students can grab whatever they're used to reading at this time from a book bag, a guided reading book, or a current personal favorite, and claim their own reading spots. You may want to bring along a few extra books with you for any early finishers—books that would appeal to a broad range of readers and are easy to get into—think graphic novels, wordless picture books, or browsable nonfiction.

Read a book to invite observations about the outdoors and launch writing

You probably have favorite books that invite readers to take a look at the outdoors, whether you are in an urban, suburban, or rural setting. Some may relate to the changing of seasons, like *Leaf Man* (Ehlert 2005), *The Snowy Day* (Keats 1962), *Snowflake Bentley* (Martin and Azarian 1998), and *My Winter City* (Gladstone and Clement 2019). A set by author–illustrator Kenard Pak—*Goodbye Autumn, Hello Winter* (2017), *Goodbye Winter, Hello Spring* (2020), and *Goodbye Summer, Hello Autumn* (2016)—might invite readers to notice the transitions between seasons in their setting.

Poetry invites us to connect with the outdoors

Poetry books, in particular, use rich language that invites us to use our senses in experiencing our surroundings and feelings they evoke. Books like *Forest Has a Song* (VanDerwater 2013), *Outside Your Window: A First Book of Nature* (Davies 2012), *Swirl by Swirl: Spirals in Nature* (Sidman 2011), and *Sharing the Seasons: A Book of Poems* (Hopkins 2010) offer poems that help us recognize our own feelings and connect to the outdoors.

You might read a poem like *Maples in October*, from Amy Ludwig VanDerwater's *Forest Has a Song* (2013), to your students. Choral reading is fun, and in this poem two maple trees talk about the signs of fall and decide that it's time to change their color. Other opportunities to read out loud together are found in *Seeds, Bees, Butterflies, and More! Poems for Two Voices* (Gerber 2013). Description in poetry invites us to measure our experiences using language— it's cold! Windy! Warm!—and notice our world using all our senses. Support your students with a note-taking chart organized by senses: I see, I feel, I hear, I touch, and I smell. Unless you have a school garden at harvest time, you should probably bring along a snack for the sense of taste.

Nature journals

Lean on the five (or four) senses again and capture observations in a nature journal on a regular basis. Keeping a journal over the course of a year will naturally invite students to notice changes. One of my favorite resources for nature journal writing are poet and author Amy Ludwig VanDerwater's videos created in collaboration with a school district and nature center in upstate New York to support student writers during the pandemic. Each provides a different prompt or question. These videos can be found at her website, https:// www.amyludwigvanderwater .com/. Another great resource for prompts is John Muir Laws' website on nature journaling, https://john muirlaws.com/. He asks students to respond to the same three: *I notice; I wonder; What does it remind me of?* Over time, these three questions become a natural lens as students

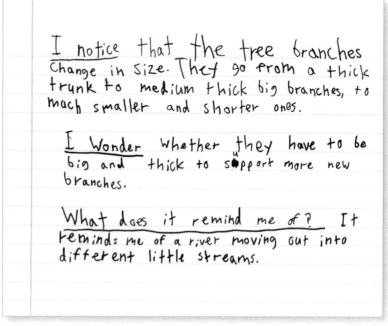

Figure 2-9 Nature Journal

Take a Walk

Once you've established some ground rules for walks regarding partners, sidewalks, boundaries, and checking in with you, your class might enjoy a weekly walk. You might take a word or letter walk, challenging your students to spot and keep a tally of the letters in their phonics program on street names and other signs. Walk and Talks are popular; use these as you might use a Turn and Talk in your classroom. You can make deliberate pairings to build conversation, literacy skills, and connections, or make matches to support social emotional learning. A senses walk with observations jotted on a clipboard could be a rich prewriting experience for poetry. Invite them on other themed walks focused on clouds, trees, patterns, puddles, and cracks, which can be launched by books like the ones below. And, as always, your students will have great ideas for walk themes and these may be the ones they become especially invested in.

A Stick Is an Excellent Thing (Singer 2012) Poems that relate to bubbles, jacks, jump ropes, balls

Everybody Needs a Rock (Baylor 1974)

Finding Wild (Lloyd 2016)

If You Find a Rock (Christian 2008)

What's in Your Pocket? Collecting Nature's Treasures (Montgomery 2021)

Wonder Walkers (Archer 2021)—asking big questions

internalize them. They can support writing in many other genres, too. And if you want to do a spontaneous dive into how senses help us experience nature, try a book like *Have You Ever Seen a Flower?* (Harris 2021) or *Wonder Walkers* (Archer 2021).

Making sense of what's outside: Field identification guides

For years a colleague walked around campus enjoying the trees, but it wasn't until our botany students created signs for each tree that she felt she had a relationship with them. Knowing the names of *things* adds to our schema and allows us to build connections and figure out relationships. My colleague might then wonder about the next tree: *This has a similar shape, is it also an oak?* She is building her knowledge about trees, which enhances her relationship with them. She confided that simply seeing the identification sign empowered her to recognize pin oaks everywhere. Field Identification guides are a genre of their own with sections, categories, and tools to help readers quickly find the answer to *what is this?* Your favorite librarian can help you gather a variety of field identification guides so that your students can analyze what makes a good one. Using a tree or bird guide as an example, they will likely notice:

- ▶ The setup of the guide: categories like geographic region, color of tree or bird, beak shape

- ▶ What information is included: categories such as sea birds, deciduous trees

- ▶ Types of images: sketches, thumbnail photographs, maps

- ▶ Brevity of the language used and specific terms.

A good place to start is with a field guide to birds or trees because birds or trees are pretty much everywhere. Help your students see the ways that guides help you narrow what you are looking at by using categories like region of the country, color, shape, and even, with birds, bird calls. Typical tree guides help you focus on the shape of the tree from a distance—pointy? round? Or the leaf arrangement and shape—alternating? pointy? round? Or the bark—rough or smooth? Search online for simple and common guides, print, and laminate them for a class set. Once students are familiar with the guides and their characteristics, they will be ready to create their own for topics like clouds,

Figure 2-10 Take a walk.

rocks, insects, and flowers. The writing of a guide can be an authentic application of new knowledge if it is part of your weather, rocks, or plants science curriculum.

Backpacks, scavenger hunts, and STEAM bins: Preparation pays off

Just as in any other area of your curriculum, finding a like-minded colleague or two interested in moving literacy outdoors will create synergy and a level of energy and support for finding ways to make things work outside. Prepping a treasure or scavenger hunt experience or a grab-and-go bag once means that several classes can use it. With their teachers on board, older students could create hunts or backpacks for younger students. For example, a fifth-grade class studying tree networks could apply their new knowledge in picking out tree books for a younger class whose science curriculum involves living things or plants. Creating a scavenger hunt related to trees, leaves, and bark is a good review tool for older students and will create shared knowledge about the school grounds and trees for the whole student population. In your own class, partners or small groups could gather a set of books for their classmates about a shared interest; this task would encourage discussion, require analysis and critique of books, and give learners agency. Finally, outdoor-themed backpacks and treasure hunts provide a fun and focused activity for events when the school community, families, and partners come together.

Scavenger/treasure hunts

With their trusty clipboards and a little planning on your part, your students will love to get outside to do a scavenger hunt. You and your students can explore your setting and develop language and vocabulary over the school year. Think about the learning opportunities in this task the way that you would for any word work in your class; you might move from using familiar and predictable words in the fall, to mixing it up and adding more challenging ones as the year progresses. Use both visual and verbal text in your lists; including both types of clues supports readers and enables them to be more independent.

An online search for examples of nature and outdoor scavenger hunts will yield endless examples if you get stuck! Try some of the ideas in the chart below (Figure 2–13) to get started; if you share initial lists with your colleagues, they may be inspired to offer up their own. If your class is enamored by these, consider having a "Treasure Hunt Thursday" every week. Treasure Hunt Tuesday works, too, although as we know, any day is a good day to get outside.

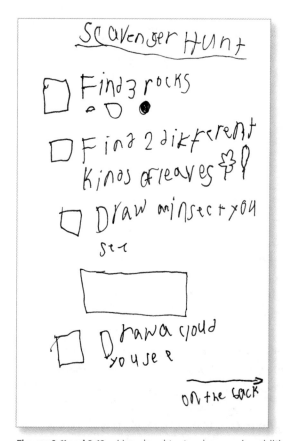
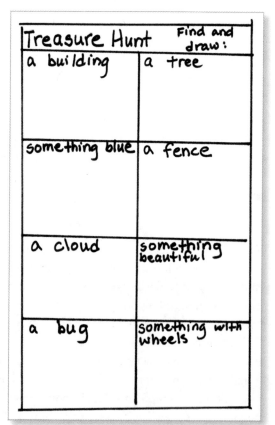

Figures 2-11 and 2-12　Use visual text or images in addition to words to support your readers. Invite students to create hunts for each other or for younger children.

Scavenger Hunts à la carte: Choose terms and items to craft hunts that will support and challenge your students.

Action words (imperatives, directions)	Items	Seasonal and other themes: Lean on specialist teachers for vocabulary and concepts your students can apply during their scavenger hunts.
• Get • Collect • Amass • Count • Find • Draw • Sketch • Outline • Diagram • Assemble • Arrange • Order • Choose	• Pebbles, rocks, stones • Sticks, twigs • Leaves • Tree • Plant • Pattern • Pine cone • Bird, feather • Insect • Pavement feature • Cloud • Building • Sign • Fence • Car, bus, subway • Bicycle • Fire hydrant • Words!	• If seasons change in your area, consider adding these to your lists. For example: leaf colors, snow or plows, weeds, flowers, buds • Art terms such as: textures (smooth, bumpy, bristly, jagged, soft, hard), shape (regular, irregular, round, square, triangular, heart-shaped), color (bright, soft, mixed, specific colors), line (thin, thick, zigzag, curvy) • Science terms could find their way into your list: identify, guess, observe, hypothesize, investigate, evidence, measure, predict, record • Weather-related items might include: puddles, clouds, snow, mud • Gardens might invite students to find seeds, weeds, flowers, vegetables, soil, worms, tools • In urban play yards or neighborhoods, students might find chalkings, painted game boundaries, cracks, insects, shapes, vehicles, signs, and more

Figure 2-13

Once they've participated in a few, invite your students to create hunts or quests for each other or for other classes. You can support this new writing task in the way that you do any new genre, with minilessons about actions, imperatives, and ways to collect evidence. Take a brainstorming walk outside and you can count on children to notice things to add to their lists that you have overlooked. Students can make these for each other as a practice run, then try partnerships between different grade levels, like book buddies. As a way to bring the outdoors inside, consider how your students might make collages out of the physical items they collect on their treasure hunts.

Figure 2-14   Art collages out of scavenger hunt finds

Figure 2-15   Student-made guide to owl feathers

Grab-and-go themed backpacks, bins, or tote bags

A busy teacher friend once told me that she dreamed of a preloaded literacy backpack she could grab to head outside with her class when the weather turned nice. In her fantasy, maybe it would relate to her curriculum, maybe not, but the books and related activities inside would help her class enjoy being outside and continue their learning. Once outside, she would pull out an engaging book, some simple supplies to launch discussion and exploration, and the tools needed to support creating, recording, and imagining. Having a backpack at the ready can set you and your students up for a predictable literacy routine that can grow and change along with your goals. One backpack for the teacher might morph into numerous backpacks shared by partners or small groups; you might eventually have enough for each student to choose an individual backpack with books and materials based on a theme like clouds or insects.

What might go in my friend's imagined backpack? Books. You might create a backpack around a theme, an author or illustrator, or one special book that your students will find immediately inspiring. There are lots of ways to go with this, as described on page 27.

Crafting Scavenger Hunts That Support and Challenge Your Learners

Just as in all literacy learning, we want our students to have successes and challenges during their year with us. As always, you'll want to consider your students' needs, but at the *beginning of the year*, your hunts might start simply, to ensure that students can follow the directions and learn the genre:

- Draw something red
- Draw a cloud
- Draw a sign
- Get 3 rocks
- Find a leaf
- Count the swings

Toward the *end of the year* they'll be ready to level up, so your language and tasks should reflect their prowess!

- Gather 3 stones with different textures
- Sketch a cloud shape
- Amass at least 5 leaves that represent different shapes and colors
- Illustrate 3 things that convey today's temperature
- Jot down 3 sounds you hear
- Identify 1 bird
- Record an observation about the playground

What else goes into the backpack? It's helpful to think of two general ideas. First, what will support literacy, literally? Be sure that you include writing implements, paper or journals, and clipboards; alternatively, you could bring the individual student materials bins (shown in Figure 2–5). Second, what will you want students to do after reading? What materials will invite you all to explore this topic in an immediate way? A cloud-themed backpack might

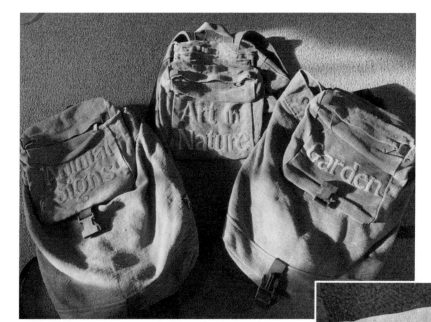

Figure 2-16

Shelburne Farms–themed
backpacks and content list

Figure 2-17

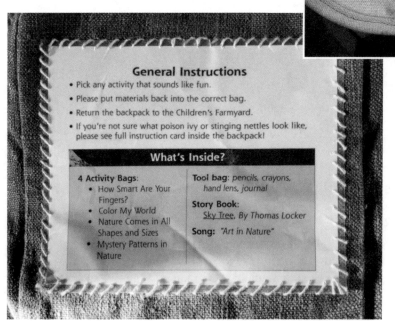

General Instructions
- Pick any activity that sounds like fun.
- Please put materials back into the correct bag.
- Return the backpack to the Children's Farmyard.
- If you're not sure what poison ivy or stinging nettles look like, please see full instruction card inside the backpack!

What's Inside?

4 Activity Bags:
- How Smart Are Your Fingers?
- Color My World
- Nature Comes in All Shapes and Sizes
- Mystery Patterns in Nature

Tool bag: pencils, crayons, hand lens, journal

Story Book: Sky Tree, By Thomas Locker

Song: "Art in Nature"

Figure 2-18

include blue construction paper, white crayons, pastels, or chalk, or even cotton balls. A rock- or stone-themed backpack could have a portable Mancala game, a hand-held magnifying lens, and a field guide for identifying stones. Think about materials that will be manageable and will help you deepen the experience. Vermont's Shelburne Farms offers backpacks for visitors to the children's farmyard that provide a similar experience. In a smart move, there is a list of the contents with just enough description for users to know what their choices are and to help users keep the right materials with the right backpack.

Getting started with grab-and-go backpacks

A natural progression involving the number of books, the number of backpacks, and a varied level of choices will set you and your class up for hours of enjoyable reading outdoors.

One book to be read aloud

To help your class understand how this might work, keep the first experience simple and in your control. Prepare a backpack that includes a touchstone book, something that relates to the outdoors and invites participation. You might pick something like Byrd Baylor's *Everybody Needs a Rock* (1974), or *If You Find a Rock* by Peggy Christian (2008). Both of these books invite listeners to think about what makes each rock special, and just about every outdoor space offers rocks to examine. If you can, include a class set of magnifying lenses and some paper on which to record your students' "rules" for which rocks to collect, just like the character in Baylor's book. Other books that would work well would be *Roxaboxen* (McLerran 1991), *Tell Me, Tree* (Gibbons 2004), *Flip, Float, Fly: Seeds on the Move* (Macken 2016), *Tiny, Perfect Things* (Clark 2018), or any book that invites students to interact with their setting. This approach is a good way to start moving outside with backpacks, as everyone is involved with the same book and activity. This will allow you to model ways of interacting with the book and environment and monitor the experience.

One theme for a set of books in one backpack: All about birds, clouds, or bugs

Once your students have had the opportunity to engage with the idea of the book backpacks outside, you might expand the experience, giving them a little more independence and personalizing the reading material. Still using one backpack, you can load it with numerous books about the same topic, which offers you a chance to think about how to meet your individual students' reading needs and interests. Create these book groupings as you would any thematic bin in your classroom library. (See Figure 2–19.) Say your theme is birds—are there nonfiction, poetry, and fiction books included? Do they range from simple to complex? Is there a variety of formats, including picture books, graphic novels, and chapter books? Will each of your readers find something for themselves? You might put students in deliberately designed partnerships or trios, with their names on a sticky note on the book cover. Consider whether they will need their materials bin or just a clipboard and stash some bird calls and

Figure 2-19

binoculars into the backpack to support their exploration. You could even begin by reading aloud one bird book to everyone before sending them off to read their assigned books.

Multiple backpacks for partners, small groups, or individuals

The two models above—one book read aloud to all, or multiple books gathered on one theme—might be enough to start with for busy teachers; there's no reason this could not be the backbone of your outdoor reading experiences for the year. Over time you may develop more themed backpacks or find a colleague who is willing to swap with you, which increases choice in terms of themes or topics in the backpacks for your students. Beyond topical themes like rocks, clouds, and birds, author and illustrator studies make great sets of books for a backpack or tote bag. What could be better for student writers than spending some time outside immersed in nonfiction genius Steve Jenkins' work, or diving into Jacqueline Woodson's powerful narratives? Once students are savvy and comfortable with outdoor procedures, invite them to grab a backpack that matches their interest, and go find their favorite spot. One might choose an author-focused pack like Lois Ehlert, and their friend might pick an owl theme. Because you know your students' social and academic needs, you can be as involved in these choices as you see fit, directing readers toward specific themes or partners, or leaving these choices up to them.

Some backpack themes and books to get you started

To circle back to my teacher friend who wanted preloaded backpacks, here are some suggestions centered on themes that could work in many school settings. The books range from classics to recently published and include fiction, nonfiction, and poetry. You'll want to see what you can find among these suggestions and add your own favorites.

Backpack Themes and Books

Birds

Mama Built a Little Nest (Ward 2014)

My Awesome Field Guide to North American Birds: Find and Identify Your Feathered Friends (Graf 2021)

Pale Male: Citizen Hawk of New York City (Schulman 2008)

Every Day Birds (VanDerwater 2016)

Exploring Birds Activity Book for Kids: 50 Creative Projects to Inspire Curiosity & Discovery (Rivers 2021)

How to Find a Bird (Ward 2020)

Counting Birds: The Idea That Helped Save Our Feathered Friends (Stemple 2018)

Bird House (Gómez 2021)

Knowing the Name of a Bird (Yolen 2020)

Hummingbird (Davies 2020)

Tiny Bird: A Hummingbird's Amazing Journey (Burleigh 2020)

Wings on the Wind: Bird Poems (Kiesler 2002)

Bring on the Birds (Stockdale 2020)

_____

Bird Identification cards (purchase commercially made or make your own based on birds in your setting)

Clipboard

Binoculars

Sidewalks

The Street Beneath My Feet (Guillain 2017)

Sidewalk Flowers (Lawson 2016)

The World from Our Driveway (Everett 2021)

Lots of playground chalk!

Magnifying lenses

Paper

Peeled crayons for rubbings

Clouds

Clouds (Rockwell 2008)

It Looked Like Spilt Milk (Shaw 1988)

Fluffy, Flat, and Wet (Rau 2006)

The Cloud Artist: A Choctaw Tale (Maret 2017)

Cloudy with a Chance of Meatballs (Barrett 1978)

Explore My World Clouds (Delano 2015)

What's the Weather? Clouds, Climate, and Global Warming (Ralston and Ralston 2021)

When Cloud Became a Cloud (Hodgson 2021)

Marshmallow Clouds (Kooser, Wanek, and Jones 2022)

_____

Clipboard

Blue construction paper

White chalk or crayon

Magnifying lenses

Cotton balls

continues

Trees & Leaves

Tell Me, Tree (Gibbons 2004)

Forest Has a Song (VanDerwater 2013)

Trees (Johnston 2021)

Because of an Acorn (Schaefer 2016)

The Wisdom of Trees: How Trees Work Together to Form a Natural Kingdom (Judge 2021)

Up in the Leaves: The True Story of the Central Park Treehouses (Boss 2018)

The Tree Lady: The True Story of How One Tree-Loving Woman Changed a City Forever (Hopkins 2013)

Celebritrees: Historic & Famous Trees of the World (Preus 2016)

The Secret Life of Trees (Butterfield 2020)

A Tree Is Nice (Udry 1987)

Leaf Man (Ehlert 2005)

Red Leaf, Yellow Leaf (Ehlert 1991)

Why Do Leaves Change Color? (Maestro 1994)

Leaves (Bodach 2018)

Tree Finder: A Manual for the Identification of Trees by their Leaves (Watts 1991)

Winter Tree Finder for Identifying Deciduous Trees in Winter (Watts and Watts 1970)

——————————

Leaf Identification cards (purchase commercially made or make your own based on trees in your setting)

Magnifying lenses

Clipboard with paper and peeled crayons for leaf rubbings

Tree Identification cards (purchase commercially made or make your own based on trees in your setting)

Clipboard

Paper and implements for sketching

Windows

The Hello, Goodbye Window (Juster 2005)

Windows (Denos and Goodale 2017)

Windows (Guest 2020)

Outside My Window (Ashman 2018)

Through the Window: Views of Marc Chagall's Life and Art (Rosenstock 2018)

Window (Arbona 2020)

Clipboard

Graph paper

Crayons, markers, or colored pencils for creating images of stained-glass windows, curtains, or other window art

Glass markers for drawing on windows, if permitted

Snow

Snowflake Bentley (Martin 1998)

Ten Ways to Hear Snow (Camper 2021)

Over and Under the Snow (Messner 2011)

Wolf in the Snow (Cordell 2017)

Lemonade in Winter: A Book About Two Kids Counting Money (Jenkins 2012)

Snow Music (Perkins 2003)

Names for Snow (Beach 2003)

Snow, *continued*

The Story of Snow: The Science of Winter's Wonder (Cassino and Nelson 2009)

My Winter City (Gladstone 2019)

Snow Day! (Laminack 2007)

Clipboard

Magnifying lenses

Black construction paper

Rocks & Stones

Stick and Stone (Ferry 2021) 3 books in this series

Everybody Needs a Rock (Baylor 1974)

If You Find a Rock (Christian 2008)

Stone Painting for Kids: Designs to Spark Your Creativity (Bac 2018)

Make Your Own Inuksuk (Wallace 2004)

All About Rocks and Minerals: An Introduction for Kids (Trusiani 2021)

What Can You Do with a Rock? (Miller 2021)

The Rock from the Sky (Klassen 2021)

A Rock Is Lively (Aston 2015)

A Stone Sat Still (Wenzel 2019)

Roxaboxen (McLerran 1991)

_____

Portable Mancala set

Stones and paint supplies (to make kindness rocks)

Egg cartons for sorting

Bees

Begin with a Bee (Ketchum et al. 2021)

Bea's Bees (Pryor 2019)

The Beeman (Krebs 2020)

Bees (Fuhr 1997)

The Honey Makers (Gibbons 2000)

If You Love Honey (Sullivan 2015)

Please Please the Bees (Kelley 2021)

Beekeepers (High 2002)

Honeybee: The Busy Life of Apis Mellifera (Fleming 2020)

Bee: Nature's Tiny Miracle (Hegarty 2016)

The Thing About Bees: A Love Letter (Larkin 2019)

_____

Chart for identifying flower sizes, and observations of bee sizes. Identify the pattern of large flower, large bee; tiny flower, tiny bee.

Garden

The Wind's Garden (Roberts 2001)

Planting the Wild Garden (Galbraith 2011)

Water, Weed, and Wait (Fine and Halpin 2010)

City Green (DiSalvo-Ryan 1994)

One Little Lot: The 1-2-3s of An Urban Garden (Mullen 2020)

Our Community Garden (Pollak 2004)

Errol's Garden (Hibbs 2019)

continues

Garden, *continued*

Flower Garden (Bunting 1994)

Dandelions: Stars in the Grass (Posada 2000)

Wanda's Roses (Brisson 1994)

The Gardener (Stewart 1997)

Garden tools

Paper and writing implements for designing a garden or creating signs for plants; depending on whether your site has gardens or land-scaped areas or container plants

Signs

Runaway Signs (Holub 2020)

Give Me a Sign! What Pictograms Tell Us Without Words (Samoyault 1997)

A Book About Signs (Weekes 2015)

I Read Signs (Hoban 1983)

We Love Reading Street Signs (Carlton 2017)

New York City Street Signs Learn to Read with Environmental Print (Carlton 2020)

STOP, WAIT, GO! Road Signs and Symbols It's Fun to Know (King 2018)

Signs in My Neighborhood (Lyons 2013)

———————————

Shape templates

Paper

Crayons/colored pencils/markers

The theme possibilities are endless, and the more you create sets of books, the more will occur to you. Be sure to solicit suggestions from your students. Here's a starting list of topics that may be a possible match for your setting:

- Bugs
- Butterflies
- Playgrounds
- Pourquoi Tales
- Puddles
- Seasons
- Shadows
- Sun
- Water

You can also take cues from what's happening at your school. One teacher tackled a multiyear construction project by gathering books and materials that created an opportunity for learning during what might otherwise have been a disruption (see Box).

Figure 2-20

What's Happening at Your School?

Let local—school and community—events guide you as you gather books and materials for your outdoor sets. Second-grade teacher Hanna Lesch is shaping a grab-and-go backpack centered on construction. Her urban school will be undergoing renovations for two years and she plans to build on her primary-grade students' interests in machinery, demolition, and tools in crafting a text set. To build on the books below, she plans to include graph paper, rulers, shape templates, small truck toys, and other manipulatives to help students explore and represent what they are observing over time. Hanna plans to make a class book based on her own photos, student writing and drawings, and captions.

The Construction Alphabet Book (Jerry Pallotta)

Construction People (Lee Bennett Hopkins, ed.) A book of poems about those who work in construction

Let's Meet a Construction Worker (Bridget Heos)

Dirt Machines: Heavy-Duty Construction Vehicles (M. Kaye David)

I Spy with My Little Eye: Construction Site (Rainbow Lark)

Alphabet Under Construction (Denise Fleming)

Construction Machines (Chris Oxlade)

Board books that provide vocabulary and clear illustrations

Goodnight, Goodnight, Construction Site (Sherry Duskey Rinker)

Construction Site Mission: Demolition! (Sherry Duskey Rinker)

Touch and Explore Construction (Stephanie Babin)

Many public librarians work hard to connect families with books using themed sets with accompanying crafts, models, toys, and other materials and redoubled these efforts during the pandemic to get books into the hands of readers. Kings County Public Library in Washington State promotes a program called *Books to Grow On*; each kit includes books, songs, and toys related to themes like *fall*, *winter*, *spiders*, and *trees*. Fletcher Free Library in Vermont developed STEAM kits with themes like bugs and backyard birds. Similar to the grab-and-go literacy backpacks, plastic bins with themed books and manipulatives is another model for how school kits could come together.

Resources

Heard, Georgia. 1999. *Awakening the Heart: Exploring Poetry in Elementary and Middle School.* Portsmouth, NH: Heinemann.

Robertson, Juliet. 2014. *Dirty Teaching: A Beginner's Guide to Learning Outdoors.* Carmarthen, Wales, UK: Independent Thinking Press.

3

STORYWALKS®

What Is a StoryWalk®?

Picture this: It's spring and everyone is eager to get outside. Your students pick up their clipboards and pencils and head out to the park next to the school. In front of a big tree is the cover of a book, *Mama Built a Little Nest* (Ward 2014), and page one is visible a few paces away, enticing students to walk along a path that will reveal page by page the ways that different birds build their nests. It's easy to imagine how this book would compel readers to look carefully at the trees and shrubs around them to see whether they could find any nests. And picture this, too: it's the pandemic, and your students are getting good at keeping six feet apart. One city school knows just how to work literature into this situation; pages from the beautiful book *The Day You Begin* (Woodson 2018) are posted six feet apart down the school hallway to the cafeteria. What could be better than a good read on your way to lunch?

What is a StoryWalk®? Invented by Anne Ferguson with the Kellogg-Hubbard Library (www.kellogghubbard.org/storywalk) in Montpelier, Vermont, StoryWalks®—simple but ingenious—invite readers to walk along a path with staked pages of an engaging book related to the setting. Like *Mama Built a Little Nest* (Ward 2014), whose exploration of birds and their nests matches up perfectly with a walk near trees, the best walk books deepen the reader's understanding of place. The cafeteria hallway is a perfect place to offer Woodson's (2018) powerful message about finding your identity in your school community even as students muster the patience to wait for lunch. You may encounter StoryWalks® by other names such as *poetry walks*, *book walks*, *story hikes*, *song walks*, and on a bike path, *story cycles*. I look forward to a story experience on a river or pond, possibly called a *story paddle*.

Figure 3-1
Pictured here are illustrations from a plant book lining a path through a park. Install your book experience on your playground, in the hallway, or elsewhere in your community.

Why a StoryWalk®?

Even before and after "social distancing" challenged all of us to be outside in safe and rewarding ways, StoryWalks® have enticed families, classes, and individuals as a perfect way to experience the outdoors together, to get some exercise, and to share the rewards that stories offer regardless of setting. A StoryWalk® at a farmers' market in Charlottetown, Prince Edward Island, features *Fresh-Picked Poetry: A Day at the Farmers' Market* (Schaub 2017). Each poem is carefully matched to its booth. The poem "Market Melody" is nailed to a wall next to the gathering place for musicians. Other poems invite shoppers to picture the farmers up at dawn, harvesting produce for market, or to inhale the scent of fresh-baked goods.

In the garden of a local elementary school, Kate Messner's *Up in the Garden and Down in the Dirt* (2015) offers readers a glimpse into those parts of the garden that we can't usually see. The illustrations take us *down* into the soil, showing us the components of the unseen garden ecosystem. Seeing both views of the garden—the visible live plants above the ground and the illustrated world below the soil—enriches our understanding of the whole garden. Whether at the farmers' market, in the garden, or in a school hallway, a StoryWalk® not only adds to the enjoyment of the moment but shows us the power of books to offer information that enhances our lived experiences. These examples, and the indoor walk showcasing *The Day You Begin* (Woodson 2018), all engage students because they speak to the moment and place, connecting reader and book in an immediate and authentic setting. Even when we reach the end, StoryWalks® have staying power because they invite readers to experience the universality that literature offers: *I see my experience in this book* and likewise, *characters in a book are having an experience similar to my own.* In other words, content shared through StoryWalks® can reflect one's own experience, but also deepen this experience through new information or perspectives.

What makes a good StoryWalk® book?

The garden, market, and "getting to know you" books in the opening paragraphs are examples of perfect picks. There are so many great books and once you and your students have the chance to try out a few you will see possibilities everywhere. In time, you and your readers will begin to approach every book through the lens of "Hmm, would THIS make a good story experience?" Here are a few ways to get you started thinking about book selection.

Look for books that might:

▶ Provide a deeper look or connection into a setting. These might be nonfiction books about ecosystems, history of a place, or characteristics of a neighborhood. Books like *Forest Has a Song* (VanDerwater 2013), *Small in the City* (Smith 2019), *Nature in the Neighborhood* (Morrison 2004), *Pale Male: Citizen Hawk of New York City* (Schulman 2008), *Up in the Leaves: The True Story of the Central Park Treehouses* (Boss 2018), and *Last Stop on Market Street* (de la Peña 2015) all offer ways to connect, wonder, and imagine in a particular setting. A state parks naturalist chose *The Lorax* (Seuss 2012) to lure those familiar with the movie into the woods for a firsthand experience with trees (bonus: a national forestry grant provided the funding).

▸ Support exploration of a curricular or social goal. Jacqueline Woodson's *The Day You Begin* (2018) or *Alma and How She Got Her Name* (Martinez-Neal 2018) help launch an inclusive tone for the school community. Walks featuring nonfiction books like *Tell Me, Tree* (Gibbons 2004), *The Thing About Bees: A Love Letter* (Larkin 2019), or *A Place for Butterflies* (Stewart 2011) offer the chance to immediately connect local surroundings with literature in the science curriculum.

▸ Offer a sense that their experience is universal. These books might present family and friends going on picnics, playing games, being with friends, facing struggles, and celebrating, all relatable for many children. Look for books like *Pie Is for Sharing* (Ledyard 2018), *Saturday* (Mora 2019), and *Big Red Lollipop* (Khan 2010).

▸ Invite readers of different ages and experiences to engage in the book, providing an experience for a broad age-range audience. Consider how a book might offer information in varying levels of depth and detail. *The Water Princess* (Verde and Badiel 2018), posted by the King County Library system in Washington State, contains a story of a child's walk with her brother that could be appreciated by preschoolers; an older child reading the book might also sense the equity issue presented about access to water. Nonfiction writer Steve Jenkins' work (see Children's Books Cited) typically includes different levels of text, from overarching, bolded questions to small captions and details. There's something for every reader.

I summarize these guidelines in the chart that follows to help you choose a book that works for your setting, your students, and your community.

Guide to Choosing a Book

Books that may	Characteristics to look for	Examples
Provide a deeper look into or connection with the setting	• Fiction or nonfiction • Relate directly to setting	• *Mama Built a Little Nest* (Ward 2014) • *Small in the City* (Smith 2019) • *Planting a Rainbow* (Ehlert 1988)
Support exploration of a curricular or social area	• Fiction or nonfiction, with a focus on academic or social curricula • Set the stage for social interactions (inclusivity) • Can be focused on a science topic, like bees	• *Alma and How She Got Her Name* (Martinez-Neal 2018) • *The Thing About Bees: A Love Letter* (Larkin 2019)
Offer a sense that the experience is universal and invites the reader to relate	• Often more storylike, enticing the reader along the reading path • Present family and friends together in lifelike episodes	• *Pie Is for Sharing* (Ledyard 2018) • *Saturday* (Mora 2019) • *Big Red Lollipop* (Khan 2010)
Invite readers of a broad age range to engage in the book	• Often fiction or nonfiction • Offer information and messages at different levels of understanding and in different ways, visually	• *The Water Princess* (Verde and Badiel 2018) • *The Gardener* (Stewart 1997)

Figure 3-2   Guide to Choosing a Book

Where to do a StoryWalk®?

Everywhere! Playgrounds, hallways, gardens, wooded areas, libraries, nurses' offices, cafeterias, and classrooms can all be the perfect setting for a special book. What could cheer up sick students better than reading *A Bad Case of Stripes* (Shannon 1998) or *Tiny Creatures: The World of Microbes* (Davies 2014) as they take a rest? *Strega Nona* (dePaola 2017) or *Before We Eat* (Brisson 2018) could make lunchtime more fun or informative, especially if there is a line. As a kindergarten teacher, I used to laminate pages from joke books and other quick reads for the walls of our classroom bathroom. Some students would undoubtedly appreciate the relevance of the popular title *Everyone Poops!* (Gomi 2001). Often the choice of site will come down to access, but if you're lucky, your colleagues and administrators will see the value in having books become integrated into physical spaces because StoryWalks® give the message that books and the written word belong everywhere.

Logistics: How to Make a StoryWalk®

▶ The book: You'll need two copies of the book, three ideally. While there are copyright restrictions for copying books, once you buy the book you can take it apart to post the pages. You will need two copies—because pictures are printed on both sides—and ideally, you'll have a third for revisiting in the classroom as a read-aloud or for students to pick up on their own. Budget considerations: the paperback version—often less expensive—is fine, as you will be taking it apart and laminating the pages. If the library owns or can purchase a copy of the book for read-alouds, you'll save there, too.

▶ Lamination: You'll want your outdoor story to withstand rain, snow, and wind. Laminate the pages with the thickest possible laminating sheets so that they don't curl, and you can use them multiple times. One librarian's signature move is to mount each illustration on cardstock to make it sturdier before laminating. And to ensure the longevity of the pages for future use, don't staple through the lamination, as rain or snow may seep in.

▶ Posting pages: You've got lots of choices here, depending on what works best for your site. Outdoor natural areas or gardens can use stakes or fences; indoor walks can be displayed on walls or bulletin boards. Sturdy wooden garden stakes or the stronger (but more expensive) green metal ones can become a part of a permanent path or be installed when you're featuring a StoryWalk®. Some setups feature a page attached to a stake or pole; others use a rectangular piece of plywood as backing support for the pages.

Figures 3-3 and 3-4 Options for your page stands can include green metal fence stakes or wooden posts, with rectangular wooden boards at the top for attaching the pages.

▶ Page height: How tall is your audience? The height of your most likely or intended audience will be important to consider, whether it's you and your colleagues setting up a walk for your students or your class designing their own StoryWalk® for others.

▶ Attaching the pages to the foundation for display: Many experienced installers swear by industrial-strength Velcro strips (fuzzy part on the stake; loops on the page). If attached to a rectangular board, large binder clips work well. Cup hooks at the top of a stake work with the hole in binder clips. Fence or wall setups can include punching a hole into the top of each page (may be reinforced with duct tape or hole reinforcers) and hung on a nail, hook, or pushpin. Think of the structures as hardware and pages as software; once you've got your foundational pieces in place, it becomes easy to swap out the pages each time you want to post a new book.

▶ Orient your audience: The great thing about StoryWalks® is that you plunge right in. You see a beautiful page that invites you to look at it, begin reading, and literally take steps to seek out the next. You may decide to post a welcoming note explaining the idea of the StoryWalk®, giving credit and brief thanks to the author, funders, or acknowledging the class who set it up. If there are numbers to follow, here's the place to let your walkers know. At the end, you might post a way for viewers to respond to their experience, particularly one created by students (see one way via QR code). This provides a feedback loop for your writers who would like to create a new one based on readers' reactions. If you have the feedback delivered to you, you'll have a chance to monitor the comments before sharing with your writers.

▶ Sharing resources/dissemination: Once you have created a walk out of a picture book or your students have written one, the lamination preserves it for use the next year, and allows you to create a reuseable resource for the entire school or even district. The story pages might be checked out of a central library for other schools or classrooms to use. After the initial energy of installing the stakes or hallway hooks, your main focus will be selecting new books for the walks.

Figure 3-5 A QR code provides a way to offer comments to the story writer from the audience.

From Reading StoryWalks® to Writing Them: Helping Students Create Their Own Story Experiences

Getting started

Once your students have experienced a few walks, they'll be eager to create their own. Ask them what they've learned about StoryWalks® in general, and which ones appealed to them specifically. To start, you might create anchor charts titled "What makes a good StoryWalk®?" followed by "Ideas." While I've included some generic ideas below, your students' lists will be based on their experiences. A starting list might include:

What Makes a Good StoryWalk®?

- Start and finish are clear
- Order of reading is clear
- Makes reader want to keep reading (cliff-hanger, interesting story, lots of information)
- Illustrations/pictures

Figure 3-6
Starting ideas to guide student writers

Next steps would include their ideas about how to achieve these goals; for example, *using numbers on each post* would make the order clear for readers. Brainstorming ideas for these general goals before writing their own will allow students to focus on the most important criteria before setting off to write their own.

What should they write?

Anything and everything. Any of the genres they are already writing in your classroom can work well as story hikes. Poetry, stories, and nonfiction are easy to picture, but with a little imagination, a relevant persuasive essay or procedural piece could work, too. Think of placing a basket of materials for a procedural walk about drawing a chalk picture, categorizing types of clouds, or identifying deciduous or coniferous trees while following the posted steps. What could be more persuasive about a topic like "kids need more time outdoors" than reasons displayed on a StoryWalk®?

Launching student-written stories

Haile Hamlett's first-grade class created an ABC book using photos that she had taken of them in the first few weeks of the school year. Each student wrote a scaffolded sentence (_____ is for _____) for their letter, inspired by the photos. Even challenging letters like Q and V did not faze these writers.

Figure 3-7   First graders post their ABC book about their school garden.

Ralph W. Witherston sat at the window looking out at the world. Ralph was a black lab who loved to read. Of course, his humans didn't know of this. He was a truly special dog.

At home, no one was up yet. This was a good time to use the computer.

He logged on to Google and searched: "How to catch squirrels." All that came up, though, was a bunch of advertisements for squirrel traps, and he had no money.

"Darn!" said Ralph, then he went over to the bookshelves to see if there were any books on squirrels.

Figures 3-8 through 3-11
Brothers Frank and Rufus plan to intrigue and support their readers.

RALPH W. WITHERSTON

a truly special dog

by Frank & Rufus D'Amore

© 2020

A simple collaborative project like the first graders' ABC book (Figure 3–7) makes sense as a first attempt. It provides a model, is an inclusive project, and it's quick from start to finish. Teachers may recognize this as a sequence similar to the *gradual release of responsibility* model (Pearson and Gallagher 1983). Because everyone experiences it at the same time, all students can learn and discuss elements of effective writing for walks that they may use later when they write partner or individual pieces.

When their school went virtual, brothers Frank and Rufus D'Amore co-wrote and published a lengthy story—*Ralph W. Witherston: A Truly Special Dog*—with a story experience in mind. Knowing ahead of time that they would be posting each page shaped many of their planning and writing discussions from characters (not too many), consideration of how much of each page should be text and how much illustration (a good balance), and discussion about how "cliff-hangers" for each page would keep readers moving from post to post. Planning for an audience motivated careful editing, too. Frank noted to Rufus, as they edited a page of their story: "No! We can't write '*muttered* Bob'! We wrote what he says in all caps!!!"

Knowing that there will be an audience is an authentic reason for writers to consider the needs of their readers. Haile's first graders decided to go over their penciled letters with markers so that everyone could see them easily. Frank and Rufus knew that they wanted their story to be interesting enough to keep the walk going. Just as with any type of writing, you will want to discuss author's craft, audience, and page layout with your students. Writing for an audience means not only anticipating your reader's experience but also poses a new challenge of how to connect your writing to the walk setting.

A StoryWalk® is a way to publish student writing

You are already finding ways for your students to publish and share their writing and now you have another—hopefully outdoor—option. Fourth-grade teacher Aziza Malik plans to have each student select a poem from their poetry-writing unit to post as a celebratory culmination. Just think of student-generated story experiences as other ways to celebrate and enjoy their finished pieces outdoors or even down long school hallways or the wall of the school facing a playground. Like special one-time events, such as an author's tea, or poetry night, a StoryWalk® could be a short-term pop-up installation presented to invited guests on a specific day. Or, like an ongoing display of published work in your classroom or school library, it might stay up for a week or longer. Your learning community can manage the logistics and scheduling as these become popular ways to acknowledge the hard work of your student writers, get kids outside, and experience new connections between writing and setting.

More StoryWalk® connections to literacy development

In addition to providing the authentic purposes for writing, revision, and editing described above, other ways to develop reading and writing strategies and skills will emerge based on your students' needs and interests.

Here are some examples:

- ► Reading aloud/fluency practice: Students who would benefit from repeated reading aloud might take groups of younger children on a guided tour of a Story-Walk®. The repeated readings to a real audience would keep the experience fresh and authentic and help build fluency and expression for the host reader. This experience allows students to practice reading aloud, with focus on fluency and prosody, with an authentic purpose. They might read to families, their favorite adults in school, younger students, or friends and classmates.

- ► Ubiquitous sticky notes: the StoryWalk® version! Public librarian Megan Estey Butterfield posted sticky note questions on some of the pages from the book *Pie Is for Sharing* (Ledyard 2018) to engage the readers in the story. Some notes ask readers to dive deeper into the story, and others ask them to apply what is happening in the story to their own lives. For example, next to a picture of the pie in

Figure 3-12 Sticky note questions on posted pages invite readers to make connections.

the picnic basket, a note invited the reader to consider "What dessert would YOU pack for a picnic?" At the end of a walk featuring *Mama Built a Little Nest* (Ward 2014), there might be hints for finding nests in nearby trees, or suggestions and materials for building your own. Teachers or older students as reading buddies could write the initial sticky notes; your own students can pose these questions for themselves or other StoryWalkers just as they might in their own reading of books.

▶ Understanding that books relate to and enhance our lives: Many teachers have favorite books and poems to help their students enjoy the days of the week (*Saturday* [Mora]); holidays (*Our Favorite Day of the Year* [Ali], *Winter Lights* [Hines]); seasons (*Forest Has A Song* [VanDerwater], *Goodbye Summer, Hello Autumn* [Pak]); and months of the year (*When the Moon Is Full: A Lunar Year* [Pollock]). Installing a walk with books like these offers opportunities for students to predict, reread, and take agency in returning to the book at appropriate times of the school day, week, month, or year.

Other forms to consider

▶ Song walks, art walks, physical education walks: The specialist teachers at your school will have great ideas for participating once the physical structures are in place. Music teacher Betsy Greene posted verses to the familiar song "The Green Grass Grows All Around" with its references to leaves, bugs, and other easily identifiable elements of nature. Once students learned the tune, the posted lyrics were there for support as they enjoyed the natural surroundings called out in the song. A physical education teacher used each stop on the walk to post a warm-up exercise and started partners at different stations to spread out the class. And what could be better than an art gallery walk in a natural or outdoor setting?

▶ Welcome to our school: School communities want to welcome families in many languages. Why not invite community members to design pages that welcome everyone back in many languages, with accompanying illustrations? These might be posted along the entry way, around the playground, or in the school lobby. One elementary principal, whose cartoon illustrations are featured in this fifth grader's introductory sign (see Figure 3–13), appreciates the power of StoryWalks® to spread foundational messages about the school experience he wants for his student population. He thinks that "a story walk allows students and teachers to be outside, in a natural setting, to learn and ask questions at a pace that truly makes sense. In a time when we are being bombarded by information, having the chance to read and learn outside is really a gift."

▶ Virtual versions of published books: These are trickier because they require permissions, but once obtained, you and your students might post one page a day

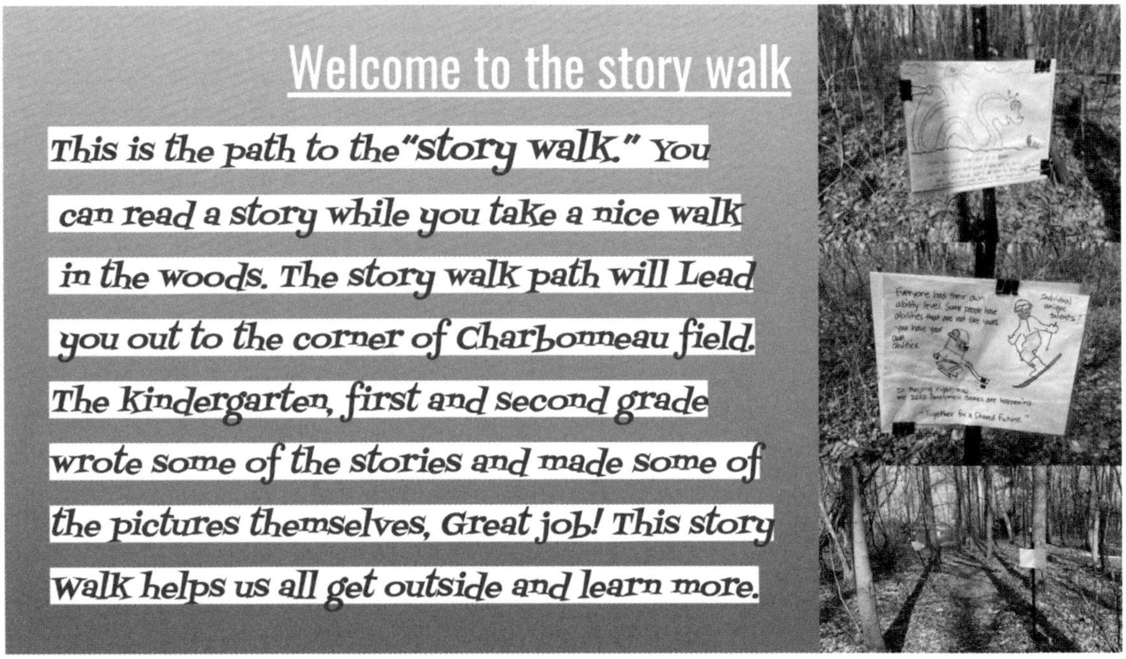

Welcome to the story walk

This is the path to the "story walk." You can read a story while you take a nice walk in the woods. The story walk path will Lead you out to the corner of Charbonneau field. The Kindergarten, first and second grade wrote some of the stories and made some of the pictures themselves, Great job! This story walk helps us all get outside and learn more.

Figure 3-13   Fifth grader Luna creates an introductory sign to the current story—a cartoon series about individual talents created by the principal.

for an ongoing story everyone can look forward to as a shared literacy routine. There's something about a slow rollout that builds anticipation! My daughters packed their own lunches, but I would cut short stories from children's magazines into paragraphs, and pack one each day alongside their sandwiches for a daily noontime rollout of a story. Charles Dickens' book *The Old Curiosity Shop*, serially published in 1840, arrived to a clamoring crowd dockside in the US via installments by boat. Got a story from your writing workshop to share with an audience? Why not post a page a day—or week—on your class newsletter, blog, or Twitter account. This way families can enjoy aspects of a StoryWalk® at home.

▶ Community partnerships: A fifth-grade class brainstormed an ingenious list of sites where they would like to see these types of story experiences: bus and subway stops, supermarkets, laundromats, and doctors' offices were popular choices. One student even insisted that those long slow airport walkways would be so much better if you could read a story on the rolling sidewalk. Community partnerships may help with funding and/or donations in terms of materials. What grocery store or transit authority could resist a thoughtfully written letter from a class with the suggestion of launching a StoryWalk® on-site? More importantly, these kinds of connections send a wraparound message about community and that literacy is everywhere and is valued.

StoryWalks® Invite Engagement

When student teachers set up a StoryWalk® displaying their third graders' drawings and diagrams to culminate a science unit, they were bowled over by the high level of engagement their students showed in reading each other's work. One noted that "the kids seemed better able to regulate themselves while outside," and another was thrilled to report that "Leah, who has been quiet and reserved from the start of the school year, was excited and even volunteered to read her page to the group." While these future teachers did not remember having this type of experience as elementary students, all are planning ways to introduce this to their schools as they enter the profession.

Resources

Need more information about StoryWalks®?

For simple overviews to share with your professional learning communities:

- ▶ FAQ and a page about StoryWalk® creator Anne Ferguson are available online at the Kellogg-Hubbard Library in Montpelier, Vermont. www.kellogghubbard .org/storywalk.

- ▶ The University of North Carolina Greensboro has a research center on Story-Walks®, including health benefits and a map of over 300 public libraries that host them.

- ▶ A free downloadable StoryWalk® is available at Curious City: Children's Book Engagement Tools, searchable online at www.curiouscitydpw.com/storywalk/.

- ▶ Use a search engine to find StoryWalks® near you. You could search for *pop-up story walks*, *library story walks*, or even *story walks near me*!

- ▶ Towns and cities can host StoryWalks®! Greenfield, Massachusetts, organized a walk with poems written about food by adult literacy learners. Albany, New York; Appleton, Wisconsin; and many other downtowns have created and hosted similar walks. An online search can provide you with details and options for community walks.

Materials

▶ Start-up materials for outside installations:

- Wood or metal stakes available at hardware stores, nursery/landscaping businesses, or lumberyards
- Attach hooks or nails to the stakes or use binder clips to hold the pages to the stake
- Alternatively, attach a square or rectangular piece of plywood to the stake and clip the pages to the board

▶ For indoor installations:

- Bulletin board strips, hooks that allow for anchoring in cement or other wall material, and large cup hooks will all work in your hallways
- Binder or clipboard clips to attach the pages to the hooks

4

WORD GARDENS

Figure 4-1

What Is a Word Garden?

If you've played around with magnetic poetry, then you've already got the idea of a word garden. Imagine the words on stones, blocks of scrap wood, painted jar lids, or other materials placed in a corner of your playground, a bed of gravel, or any available space. The words might be painted, etched, or written on the stones with chalk or a marker—the result provides many options for wordplay and learning. Like magnetic poetry, students enjoy moving these words around, but word gardens invite participation far beyond the physical task. Your students can leave messages, create poetry, start a discussion, make a joke, and just about everything else you can do with words. Deciding which words go together allows students to generate ideas, but they also delight in finding poetry, humor, and thoughts from the words that are serendipitously next to each other, creating found poetry.

The Power of a Word Garden

Figure 4-2 A little word stone humor

On the college campus where I teach, our Word Garden is set on a circular bed of gravel in a space surrounded by a hedge of flowering shrubs and trees. The 400 words, etched onto stones, reflect the pulse of our campus community; we find poems, messages, and even jokes like the numerical one in Figure 4–2.

Birthday wishes, poetry, and powerful directives such as *occupy library* and *end hunger* pop up daily. Professors hold classes in the Word Garden, and incorporate the stones into discussions, asking students to pick up a word that reflects their current thinking about a topic, or one that describes a success or challenge, as ways to begin a bigger conversation. The word stones often serve as physical props for icebreakers and to help everyone review prior learning. Our preservice student teachers host local classes of K–12 students on campus and design numerous ways for them to interact with the words. For example, we observe children creating stories, counting out the syllables for haiku, choosing words that represent an idea new to them, and finding word families, among other linguistic challenges. Inspired by their visits, many elementary teachers create word gardens at their own schools; they design ingenious ways for their students to connect with their curriculum. If you're ready to launch a word garden, here are some suggestions for getting started.

Logistics: How to Make a Word Garden

Making the stones

The beauty of a word garden is that once you have a space, you can launch one simply by finding smooth stones, pieces of wood (sanded), metal jar lids, other smooth surfaces, and a box of chalk. Because chalk is a temporary medium, it offers the benefit of allowing students to think of new words. You might keep a master list of words related to your curriculum and invite students to add more. If it rains, they will be practicing spelling and handwriting by rewriting their favorite words! An added benefit of chalk is that it is erasable and forgiving of mistakes. Other mediums work too and are more permanent; some schools have success-fully used permanent markers and others have used paint covered with a coating of shellac for durability. Jar lids with a coat of paint can provide colorful backdrops for words written with bright colored markers. For etched or sandblasted stone words, schools have leaned on

Figure 4-3   Word stones can be made using blocks of wood or painted jar lids, with letters written in permanent marker.

PTAs and other funding sources through community partnerships, "buy a word" campaigns, and donations from businesses and stores. Circling back to magnetic words, you might use magnetic strips and markers as rough drafts for your physically bigger word gardens, inviting your students to make suggestions that the whole class can discuss before committing to larger, more permanent versions.

Beyond the words themselves: Adding visual cues to strengthen meaning

Making or planning word stones can be an opportunity for learning about graphic design. Your students can probably describe some of their favorite logos, icons, and T-shirts. Ask them which fonts catch their eye. Which fonts might they use to convey scary Halloween words? To create a mood? They probably already know that a message in all capital letters implies shouting—how might a particular font help convey the meaning of *whisper* on a word stone? The size of the word can also send a message; if students fill the whole space of a stone with the word *large* and *tiny* might be found in a small corner of the stone, they begin to see the artistic and symbolic power of visual literacy. You might use books featuring concrete poetry like *Meow Ruff* (Sidman 2006) or *A Poke in the I* (Janeczko 2001) to help students get a sense of how these decisions support meaning. Color wheels, font charts, and other tools of graphic design will enable your students to study all the variables that visual artists consider to grab our attention and send a message.

Figures 4-4 through 4-7   Gold paint is used to emphasize the meaning of the word *dazzle*. *Kindness* and *love* include a red heart to emphasize the meaning of the words. The spirals added to *twist* and the angle of the letters in *lean* make each word's meaning instantly clear.

Choosing the words

Your collection of words will be shaped by your curricular goals and participants. While your collection will grow as you use it, your team or school may want to begin by defining a core set of words that works well for a variety of purposes, and plan for additional sets that are more specific to an area of the curriculum. The table on the next page provides a few tips to get the most out of your words:

Story Stones: Pictures as Text

Building on the adage *a picture is worth a thousand words*, the Memphis Botanic Gardens offers visitors a pouch with Story Stones. These are stones with images rather than words that can be used to encourage and support language play. You might provide stones with images such as a sun, a tree, and a person to prompt stories, sentences, and launching points for conversations. Discussions with students about creating these stones could include minilessons about the clarity and power of icons, symbols, and emojis to convey ideas.

1 Words that represent languages of your student population and school community

2 Words that are foundational and will be used heavily:

- prefixes and suffixes
- word study curriculum
- high-frequency, "glue" words

3 Words that are versatile and have more than one meaning:

- You'll want lots of verbs!

4 Words that are specific to your curriculum, vision, or environment:

- social studies/science unit vocabulary
- words from read-alouds or group books
- words for science like *data, observe, idea, notes, cause, effect, evidence*
- a butterfly unit might include *chrysalis, wings, cocoon, frass, Monarch, life, cycle*
- the Highlights Foundation's Word Garden (at their Writers' Retreat) includes words of inspiration for their authors: *ogre, twist, fairy*

5 Solicit ideas for words from any special area teachers.

- art: *texture, shape, color, line, composition*
- music: *beat, note, melody, harmony, lyrics*
- physical education: *stamina, stretch, jump, hop, skip, run*
- guidance: *mindful, Zen, kind, dialogue, community*

(6) Words from the broader community or setting of your school that invite connections:

- words that point to unique features of your setting, or familiar place names
- words that reflect characteristics of your community
- place-based and inspired words: *lake, city, NOLA, skate park, little library*
- words brought from home and the community into school: *bodega, belong, family, parade*

Figure 4-8   Guidelines for choosing words for your word garden

Considering space and scale: Making the words small and the word garden portable

If a permanent space is not an option at your school, consider creating a mobile one, with stones stored and at the ready in a communal wagon. A wagon like this is begging for a painted name like "Words in Motion" or "Words in Action"! Students can wheel it out for an hour or a day or pull it into the rug area of your classroom. Do individual, partner, or small-group-sized word gardens make sense for you? One teacher creates mini word gardens with wooden framed boxes available at craft stores; another recognized this same potential in cardboard plant boxes from a garden supply store.

Curricular Explorations in a Word Garden

Once you have a beginning set of words, you're ready to use your word garden as an instructional strategy. There's no doubt that you will find numerous ways to encourage your students to use the words in their learning. But if you need some ideas to get started, here are some examples of the ways that teachers have used word gardens to focus on word work, guidance concepts, literature, science vocabulary, and poetry, among others.

Figure 4-9   Cardboard or wooden framed boxes can be used as mini-word gardens right in the classroom. The one shown here is approximately 15" by 15".

Word work in the garden

A word garden, because it is made up of words, can be the perfect place for word study and wordplay. Much of the word work you do in your classroom can take place in a word garden, along with the added benefits of being outdoors and the chance for students to move around. Once you and your grade-level team have created the stones with words from your phonics or word study curriculum, word sorts like patterns, syllables, and concepts can be done with stones. Meghan Feenan, a middle grades special educator, likes to use alphabet stones to help students develop letter recognition; they can also spell their own name and those of their classmates and friends. Each stone has a letter on it, allowing children who are beginning to create letter strings to participate in a word garden even before they can read words. A primary-grade teacher in upstate New York uses a word garden as reinforcement for her students who are working to master sight words, and shares that painting and writing on the stones is good fine motor practice for them, too. At another school, teachers paint the words on stones using a distinct color for verbs, nouns, and adjectives to support student learning about parts of speech.

Figures 4-10 and 4-11   Letters written with permanent markers, words painted with acrylic paint and covered with shellac, words painted with tempera

Alphabet Stones

You might write capital letters on one side and lower case on the other; you'll want to make multiples of each letter. While the makers of Scrabble or Bananagrams must have a formula for the frequency of various letters, a great place to start is with the names on your class list and add letters as needed by your writers. River stones available in the big box hardware stores or wood blocks work well for these with temporary or permanent markers. A few quick minilessons on using the materials and your students can start making the letters they need. First-grade teacher Michelle Jacobs creates a small set of letter stones for each student and uses them to guide work in word building and phoneme manipulation.

Stone word walls

Make stone words that reflect your classroom word walls for read-alouds, group books, and other areas of the curriculum. You may be using word walls in your classroom, featuring groups of words that are related to class read-alouds, group books, or social studies and science units. These words typically highlight important concepts being discussed and provide visual access and support to students in their writing. Vocabulary words specific to units of study, word patterns, high-frequency lists, and student interests can also easily take the form of word stones. It's easy to imagine *hungry*, *butterfly*, and *collage* supporting discussion of and response to Eric Carle's classic picture book *The Very Hungry Caterpillar* (2009); recent Newbery Award winner *Merci Suárez Changes Gears* (Medina 2018) might inspire words like *bicycle*, *bully*, and *culture*. Words that are identified in specific books then become stones that are part of the word bank in the garden, available for future wordplay and writing.

Poetry

Word gardens are a perfect match for poetry writing. If you are writing words with chalk or paint, then your poets can expand the selection of words by adding words they choose as they write their poems. A different type of writing challenge can be to craft images and lines only from words that are right there in front of you. You might prompt students to see

Figure 4-12 Students identify and create word stones for a mini–word garden after discussing the important ideas in *The Hunger Games.*

Ways to Think About Poetry and Language Play in a Word Garden

In addition to haiku and other prescribed forms of poetry, students could write list and story poems, and play with metaphors, similes, and alliteration.

Figures 4-13 and 4-14
Haiku captured in stones; using fingers to count syllables; an alliterative birthday greeting

the possibilities in the word stones: Where might the words *gnome*, *poncho*, or *rumble* lead your mind? Is there a "found" line already set up in stones that you find inspiring? What might you add to it to make it your own? Teachers often encourage students to create poems individually, in pairs, or in small groups, because partner work invites conversations about language.

Students talking through word choices hear the words and rhythm aloud. In her book about teaching and writing poetry, *Poems Are Teachers: How Studying Poetry Strengthens Writing in All Genres*, Amy Ludwig VanDerwater (2018) writes about two organizational structures in poetry—*story* and *list*—that we can help students use in their poems. If your poetry work includes studying structural patterns like *list poems* or haiku based on a syllabic structure, these are easily explored with words already in the word garden. You might launch poetry in a word garden using some of these ideas.

Comprehension

Word stones are great tools for working on comprehension, too. A second-grade teacher helps each of her students create a set of three word stones labeled *B, M,* and *E,* to represent *Beginning, Middle,* and *End.* During and after read-alouds she engages the children in discussion, using the stones as prompts in identifying different parts of the story. She also challenges them to retell stories using word stones that say *main idea* and *supporting detail.*

Make science connections in the word garden

One city school in Vermont placed a word garden in a corner of the play yard next to raised garden beds to create inspiration for science notebook writing. The science coach selected the words she wanted students to use as a springboard for observations: *data, observe, seeds,* and *hypothesis* are found among other more common and versatile high-frequency words to support student thinking and writing. Students chalked additional words onto stones as they

Figure 4-15
Science terms make good word stones.

wrote about their observations. Because the word stones were outside near the raised beds, they served as a word wall for brainstorming science notebook writing.

Other possibilities for science words might stem from the crosscutting concepts identified by the Next Generation Science Standards. These seven concepts (*pattern, cause and effect, structure and function, scale, energy and matter, systems, stability and change*) could form headers for lists or take the center of a web of related words that students generate. A similar challenge could feature descriptive words for each of the five senses: *taste, sound, sight, touch,* and *smell*.

Your grade-level teams or professional learning communities might brainstorm word banks like the one below around common curricular topics studied at your school. Creating or expanding such lists with students could become an introduction to or review of important vocabulary and concepts, which gives them agency in determining importance.

Plants	Habitats	Inquiry Practices
stem	ocean	notes
seed	coral reef	observe
leaf	desert	hypothesis
petal	forest	diagram
photosynthesis	marsh	table
energy	bog	graph
water	rain forest	question
soil	grassland	data
cell	climate	evidence
color	tundra	try
pollen	Arctic	observe
pollinator		notice

Figure 4-16   Words related to science units of study

Social studies in the word garden

Any social studies topic can be explored using a word garden, whether the curriculum is prescribed or emergent. A history-based curriculum might inspire a garden featuring events, concepts, and vocabulary that invites students to match up the ideas represented by words on stones. The teachers at Ford Elementary School, in Acworth, Georgia, created a word garden they call Stepping Stones to Freedom, to engage their fourth- and fifth-grade students in the district social studies and history curriculum. Large boulders, etched with significant places in the Revolutionary War, are placed chronologically along a path. Smaller stones are painted with the names of people who played significant roles, and another set of stones has conceptual vocabulary important to this curricular topic. Students helped select the events, concepts, and people for the initial installation, discussing which should be included. As they walk along the path, students apply what they are learning in their studies by grouping the stones and explaining their reasoning. For example, students might place the stone *freedom* and another, *George Washington*, next to the boulder etched with *Valley Forge*. (See Figures 4–17 through 4–19 on the next page.)

A common social studies unit for early elementary grades is *community*, with a focus on important *institutions* in a city or town, the *services* provided, and the *roles* that people play. Together with your students, you might add stones to your garden identifying these three groups and related vocabulary words. Stable large stones for the institutions and smaller ones for the services and roles would enable students to physically match the ideas and concepts. With chalk or paint, they could add new ones as the unit progresses.

Conceptually based curricular themes, such as *change*, *social justice*, or *civil rights*, could invite students to create word stones. One upper elementary teacher is planning to use heroes from the We the Future project as springboards for learning about such current societal challenges as disability, voting, civil rights, and climate justice, among others. These concerns—together with those identified by students—could form the touchstones along a path or in a word garden. Students can create stones for significant dates, people, and ideas as they develop schema for understanding such important work and learn to articulate the connections they are making.

Other connections: Guidance

At one elementary school, a guidance counselor's purpose for the word garden is a "Zen space for children." Her goal is to create a place for students to get outside and connect with nature in a meaningful way. Discussions with fifth graders end with each student contributing a word that has the potential to spark an idea when others read it. The fifth graders' brainstorm list generated words such as *chill*, *Zen*, *family*, *peaceful*, and *nature*. These word choices offer the counselor and students a chance to launch a discussion that goes well beyond the confines of a garden, such as considering the question "What does *peace* mean to you?" (See Figure 4–20.)

Figures 4–17, 4–18, and 4–19
Events, people, and concepts selected by fifth-grade students as key in their study of the American Revolution. Students provide guided walks along the "Path to Freedom," placing relevant stones along the way.

Figure 4-20   Students identify words for use in guidance discussions.

Kindness rocks!

Join the trend of spreading kind messages in the form of rocks. While it's easy to search online for specifics, ideas, and even templates, essentially students paint cheery messages and place the stones in random—or deliberate—places around school or the community to brighten someone's day. The recipient can ponder the message and keep the stone or pass it along to the next passerby.

Last Words

While there are many ways to use a word garden in literacy learning, perhaps some of the most surprising and strongest arguments are about building a sense of school community and moving beyond age or grade-level curricula. A word garden can be a space in the school open to all students, sending the message that literacy and wordplay are for everyone. Fifth graders can have fun with the alphabet, and conversely, budding readers can enjoy seeing how the older ones "write" with the stones. Schools often set up reading buddy pairs of primary- and upper-grade students, and word gardens can invite students of different ages to craft together. If you're able to make (or take) a word garden outside, wordplay becomes an option at recess and provides an open-ended experience. Where swings and slides have a

Figure 4-21   Shape your word garden with your purposes and student population in mind.

finite set of ways children can interact with them, moveable words and letters can offer infinite possibilities for expression and exploration. The results may even give a glimpse into what's on the mind of your school community. One principal explained that her school envisioned the word garden as a fun, creative, and kid-driven way to promote literacy. She likes that students use it before and after school and during recess to create whatever they wish. Word gardens provide a way for everyone at your school, including staff, visitors, students, and administration, to contribute thoughts to a shared blank palette.

Experiences in word gardens are limitless. Physically lifting and moving the words around is fun and compelling. It provides agency for children while simultaneously enabling them to use language in novel ways. As part of the curriculum, connecting abstract thinking with physical tasks can invite powerful investment in a learning experience. Observing her students moving the stones along the Stepping Stones to Freedom path, fourth-grade teacher Dreena Varghese noted that her students were more engaged, articulate, and excited about linking historical concepts, people, and events together than in earlier paper and pencil tasks. Word gardens are engaging and adaptable learning spaces that are easily created and allow teachers to structure experiences that help students meet curricular goals.

Word Garden to Go

Special educator Meghan Feenan knew that her first through third graders would love the appeal of moving stones around to make their word work come alive. Her teaching plans consistently include movement, manipulatives, and individualized tasks. Using her district's word study program, she made word stones of base words and suffixes for her students to sort as they learned various spelling patterns. Concerned that the word stones would disappear if she left them outside, she found baskets to house them. Each time they meet, students help carry a set of stones out to the blacktop. In winter, Meghan transforms her classroom rug area into an indoor word garden.

Resources

Children's picture books are great places to launch discussions about words, as their limited pages mean that the authors think hard about how best to convey ideas. Books specifically about words and word choices can help your students think carefully and playfully about their own word stones. Here are a few suggestions to get you started talking about words and even how to have fun with writing them so that they *show* what they mean like the examples in books of concrete poetry.

Max's Words (Banks)

The Right Word: Roget and His Thesaurus (Bryant)

A River of Words (Bryant)

Shout! Shout it Out! (Fleming)

Flicker Flash (Graham) concrete poetry

Splish Splash (Graham and Scott) concrete poetry

Little Red Writing (Holub)

A Poke in the I (Janeczko) concrete poetry

The Wordy Book (Paschkis)

The Word Collector (Reynolds)

16 Words: William Carlos Williams and "The Red Wheelbarrow" (Rogers)

The Boy Who Loved Words (Schotter)

Meow Ruff (Sidman) concrete poetry

A Walk in the Words (Talbott)

Lexie the Word Wrangler (Van Slyke)

Resources for making the word stones

Figure 4-22 Stones and markers are all you need to make your own word stones.

For writing

Chalk

Sharpies

Foamies markers

Acrylic paints (can use markers over a base coat of paint)

Tempera paints

Shellac, Mod Podge, or some sort of waterproof sealer

For the stones—try for a variety of sizes

River stones (available at big box hardware stores or landscape/nursery businesses)

Smooth stones collected where available

Metal jar lids

Blocks of wood

Cardboard boxes ranging in size (for indoor spaces or temporary outdoor ones)

5

SHOW US A SIGN!

Students Use Signs to Solve Problems and Interpret Their World

Why Study Signage?

Even before they can read words, your students know that octagonal red signs mean *stop*. We teach children waiting to cross the street to look for the white or green walking figure as their cue to step into the crosswalk. Do they wonder what happened in your neighborhood before they lived there? Historic markers provide details that help us connect the present with the past. Maps help us get where we want to go. From the time we are young, signs are a part of our visual landscape and help us mediate our daily lives. In fact, they *sign*al to us where to go, what to do, when something will happen, and help us develop a deeper understanding of an event or place. Creating signage requires our young writers to consider audience, purpose, and voice, and make decisions about using tools of visual literacy such as icons, arrows, bullets, maps, and other types of graphic design elements to communicate effectively and efficiently. Since many of these are already a part of your literacy curriculum, making signs provides an engaging opportunity to apply these writing techniques in authentic ways. Studying signage as a genre requires readers to figure out the message created by a combination of words and images. It's also a great way for your writers to use short text to problem solve about purpose and think carefully about ways to reach their audience. Because signs are relatively short, involve graphic elements and images, and are used for authentic purposes in familiar settings, studying and creating signs offers multiple entry points for students. Not only will making signs provide students with new literacy experiences, doing so will also empower them to contribute to their school community in authentic and *significant* ways.

Signs help solve problems

To help your students see the purpose of signs, start by getting them thinking about what would happen if there were no signs. Joan Holub's picture book *Runaway Signs* (2020) is a humorous take on just such a scenario. When the signs take a vacation, chaos reigns: no one knows where it is safe to cross the street, where the library is, when the stores are open, and even the road crew can't find where to do their *road work*. Predictably, the only sign that won't take a break is *CAUTION*! You can set up the same concept by asking what would happen in your school if all the signs went on vacation or there were no signs. Perhaps they have all memorized where the gym, learning center, and health office are, but what about a visitor or new student?

It always makes sense to immerse students in a new genre before we ask them to write in it, and this is easy to do right away as schools are full of signs. Go on a sign walk; explore your classroom, hallway, or school with your class to notice signs. Because sign makers anticipate questions, help your students figure out which question each sign answers. You could help them start by listing the following.

- ▶ Signs for room names or supply labels answer: *What is this?*

- ▶ Signs with school rules or classroom norms answer: *How are people supposed to act here?*

- ▶ Signs like EXIT or *Keep Right on the Stairs* answer: *Where do I go?*

- ▶ Signs like *Family/Teacher Conferences next week* and *Poetry Breakfast on Monday* answer: *What special event is coming and when will it happen?*

Once your students begin to notice signs, you can help them dig deeper and identify both the purpose of each sign and how the message is conveyed. You might ask them questions like, "Are the signs long or short?" or "What symbols or pictures do they use?" They'll be ready to sort signs into the types of signage described next.

Meaning is created by words and symbols

After your students learn that different signs address different purposes, challenge them to think like interpretive and graphic designers do. These professionals consider how the purpose of the sign determines its placement, language, and graphic elements. It is no accident that STOP signs are bright red, always the same octagonal shape, and placed within the eye range of pedestrians, cyclists, and drivers. Sign makers also use words and symbols to get the point across quickly and to a broad audience. Studying child-friendly websites is one way to note how website designers use color, font, and placement on a screen for emphasis, meaning, and navigation. Signage as a genre offers a chance to consider these tools of communication because signs are found everywhere, and many visual elements, like the familiar circular *forbidden* symbol, are universally understood.

Figure 5-1

Steve Moline (1995), in *I See What You Mean: Visual Literacy K–8*, makes a distinction between *verbal text*—words—and *visual text*—visual elements such as maps, arrows, and graphic design tools. In effective signage, both are needed because verbal and visual text work together to convey a complete message. Ask your students to consider a sign like the one in Figure 5–2. Ask what the words say, and what the image tells them. What is the complete message? The meaning—that this learning garden is wheelchair accessible—is conveyed clearly and efficiently by the words and images working together.

Finding Signs in Picture Books

Because our society uses signs to help us navigate communal spaces, it's easy to find them everywhere. A sign walk makes sense as a first step so your students can explore signage in an authentic, firsthand way. Next, gather some picture books that feature signs. For younger children, it's a natural step toward understanding that books can represent their world. While there will be many familiar signs, there will also be some unfamiliar ones that set up a perfect discussion about the setting and purpose of each sign. Do you have a *railroad crossing* sign in your community? One that warns *cattle guard*? How about *slow* or *bump*? Where might those help solve problems? Asking students about both familiar and unfamiliar signs will help them see relationships between places, problems, and solutions.

A beginning list of books about signs:

We Love Reading Street Signs (Dustin Lee Carlton)

New York City Street Signs: Learn to Read with Environmental Print (Dustin Lee Carlton)

Runaway Signs (Joan Holub)

I Read Symbols (Tana Hoban)

I Read Signs (Tana Hoban)

Stop, Wait, Go! Road Signs and Symbols It's Fun to Know (Nancy King)

Signs in My Neighborhood (Shelly Lyons)

Give Me A Sign! What Pictograms Tell Us Without Words (Tiphaine Samoyault)

A Book About Signs (Russell Weekes)

Figure 5-2   This sign conveys its meaning using words and images working together.

In many ways, effective signage is like a page in a great picture book. Like the *Learning Garden* sign, the words and pictures work together to tell a complete story. You might try focusing on this complementary relationship during a read-aloud of just about any picture book, inviting readers to cover up words and read the pictures, and then do the reverse. What does each element tell? Together, what is the message? Try this out with a book like *A Seed Is Sleepy* (Aston 2007). Each page presents a statement, beginning with "A seed is . . ." followed by an adjective such as *secretive* on one page, or *fruitful* on another. The word tells us the main idea; the illustrations show us all the different ways that plants are secretive: hiding in pods or revealing their blossoms only once every ten years. The word—or verbal text—*fruitful* is made more meaningful by the gorgeous illustrations presenting a varied range of fruit, from coffee beans to strawberries. Just about any picture book on your shelf provides the chance to discuss how the words and illustrations work together to offer the reader a complete message. The same is true of effective signs.

Types of signs

There are different ways to categorize signage, but many sign designers group them in three ways: *regulatory* signs that present rules, *wayfaring* signs that help you find your way, and *interpretive* signs to help you understand and connect with a place. I like to use a model with six distinct types of signs within those three groups; your students will be familiar with many of these and you can use all six or select the ones you think fit your students, setting, and purpose. Figure 5–3 presents examples and definitions for six common types of signs used for regulatory, wayfaring, and interpretive purposes.

Six types of signs: Each solves a problem

Entry: These signs announce that you have arrived at your destination! KESTREL SCHOOL, COMMUNITY GARDEN, and 23rd STREET GROCERY are all considered entry signs. Some sign designers consider exit markers in this category as well, such as the ones that remind you that *You Are Leaving . . . Come Again Soon!* These are *wayfaring* signs because they help you find your way.

Identification: If one of your literacy practices is to label all the materials in your room, you are already using identification signs. Think labels like *scissors, Unifix cubes, nonfiction* that help you learn the name or location of an item. Identification signs can label classrooms and other specific-purpose rooms like the *cafeteria* or *restroom*. Identification signs can let us know the names of plants in gardens or produce in grocery stores. That's how I learned to recognize ugli fruit and star fruit!

Six Types of Signs

Sign category	Show an example like this	Elicit the purpose of the sign or identify the problem it solves. Ask *What does this sign help us know?*
Entry		*Where do I enter or leave? What is this place?* Shows where to enter or exit. Often the title of a place (classroom, school, garden).
Orientation		*Where am I? How do I get there?* These are often called *wayfaring* signs, because they help you find your way. These might include maps, paths, and arrows.
Identification		*What is this?* Identification signs provide the name of an object or place. Classroom labels on materials are identification signs.

continues

Six Types of Signs

Sign category	Show an example like this	Elicit the purpose of the sign or identify the problem it solves. Ask *What does this sign help us know?*
Interpretive		*What's going on here?* These signs offer deeper, richer information about the setting and specific projects. They include varied types of text such as symbols, diagrams, and other elements of visual literacy to help convey the message.
Regulatory (or *rules*)		*What's OK to do here? How should I behave?* Shares any rules or prohibitions in a positive and constructive way. (*Please leave the flowers here for others to enjoy. Walk in the hall.*)
Temporary		*What's going on now? Anything special I shouldn't miss?* Promotes temporary or current exhibit or display. *Pizza garden now ripe! Poetry walk-up this week only! Wednesday: Tryouts for* Annie!

Figure 5-3 Six Types of Signs

Orientation: When you visit somewhere for the first time, you rely on orientation signs to help you get where you're going. Visitors to your school look for cues to get to the front office, library, or specific classrooms. Arrows, maps, and diagrams help you know immediately whether you're on the right track. *Orientation* signs are another type of *wayfaring* sign.

Regulatory: These are the very familiar guidelines or rules that help everyone have a safe and enjoyable experience. Students often help create norms or rules for their own learning community, and they're quick to recognize that other settings have these too. Perhaps at a zoo they've noted that only the zookeepers can feed the animals. They learn that a bubble gum machine, parking meter, or laundromat washing machine may only accept quarters. And, in recent years, they've encountered regulatory signs that indicate where they are expected to wear a protective mask.

Temporary: These signs announce an upcoming event or something seasonal. We see signs about holiday concerts, meetings, or tryouts for the school play. If there is a wet floor, we might encounter a yellow cautionary board urging us to walk carefully until it dries.

Interpretive: These signs help visitors or classmates make a personal connection to a place or event. You might see these at museums, parks, and historical sites. They hold potential for short and powerful writing and have very specific guidelines about voice, content, visual elements, and design to convey a message effectively. These deserve their own section and will be explored later in this chapter.

Beyond the sign walk: Students as sign creators

Ready to start creating signs? Try this sequence of steps I used in working with a third grade to create signage for their school garden:

▶ First, create slides or examples that represent each type of sign with its name.

▶ Show each example and elicit definitions and guesses from your students about its purpose. Lean on Figure 5–4 and adapt for your students and setting.

▶ Next, set them up with a clipboard and a chart providing the six types of signs and send them off to find a local example in your classroom, school, or setting.

Once students have a sense of the purpose for each type of sign, they're set to address whatever problems signs can help solve! This is where you can work with your school community to determine where signs might be useful. In late spring, one second-grade teacher invited her current class to make signs for her incoming second graders, sharing their expertise about second grade and the classroom they had lived and learned in all year long. One team made orientation signs for the classroom library, identifying which section contained a specific genre. Another group freshened and replaced identification signs for materials, and a third group created an interpretive panel about the different curriculum units in store for next year's class. After a playground renovation, two fifth grades collaborated on new signage to make the inauguration go smoothly, addressing new traffic patterns and safety rules like *up the ladder; down the slide*. Empowering the students to study potential problems and create the signage also meant that they were sharing authority and agency in how the new playground would be used. In our third-grade garden project, the students were concerned about how to help summer volunteers working in the school garden know what to do. They spent time in the garden taking notes on which types of signs might be useful and then returned to the classroom to brainstorm questions and problems that signs could solve, including these:

- ▶ What is growing here?

- ▶ What is the garden for?

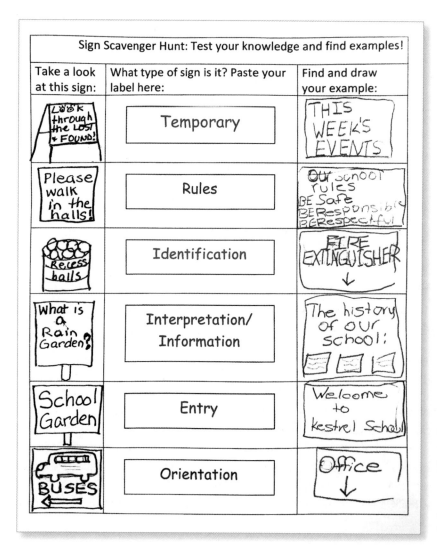

Figure 5-4
Sign Scavenger Hunt Worksheet: We provided preprinted labels with each sign type printed in a different color. As a review, students identified the provided sign images in the left column by placing the correct label in the middle column. Then they went on a sign hunt to find and draw local examples of each type of sign.

- ► Where is the equipment?

- ► What are the tasks?

- ► What if people walk on the beds?

Visual elements that create a good sign

In preparation for drafting the actual signs, students might take another look at existing school signage with a critical eye. Encourage them to observe and then use the following variables in creating their own signs.

Color: Which colors will catch a reader's attention? A color wheel is a useful tool for contrasts and complementary colors. Students find that a combination of orange and blue is eye-catching; the main idea and background might be colored with complementary colors. One third-grade student deep into the inner workings of compost explained, "I drew my compost sign in brown and green, because those are the colors of the brown for carbon and green for nitrogen." Another group chose turquoise and

Figure 5-5
Brainstorming problems that signs could help solve in the school garden

orange as the border for their sign "because those colors fight with each other and we want to grab attention." A resource like the art teacher or web designer could help students consider color choices; just about any appropriate website offers lots to talk about in terms of color.

Font Style and Size: Use a clear and legible font; fussy and fancy fonts may detract from the message. After a minilesson about how to choose fonts that help readers, one third-grade sign maker debated about using the letter *a* as "most kids write it" or the form *a* that is more commonly seen in books students read. Experiment with how large the words should be in their intended spot. Determine whether all words should be the same size or whether some should be larger or smaller. Remember that at least in social media, words in all capitals imply shouting; sometimes this might be the way to go, particularly when the sign is about safety. If the signs have sentences, then all caps makes for challenging reading and students should be encouraged to use conventional upper and lower case letters. Concern with authentic purposes and an awareness of sign readers' needs help drive writers' choices.

Images and Symbols: Is there a symbol or picture that will help convey the message? Like the wheelchair image that means *wheelchair accessible* in Figure 5–2, other universal symbols like the three arrows in *reduce, reuse, recycle* signs will be the most efficient way to get the message across. You might use a resource like Tanny McGregor's book (2019), *Ink & Ideas: Sketchnotes for Engagement, Comprehension, and Thinking,* for practice in using symbols and images to convey meaning. Ask your students to consider which images or drawings would help clarify their point. Third grader Cortina added shoes to her regulatory sign about where to walk in the garden.

Voice and Tone: What is the right tone for the sign? Just like classroom norms, regulatory signs that are positive and constructive—like Cortina's *Walk on Woodchips*—may have a better chance at compliance, since they give the reader a clear vision of how to behave. Cortina's original draft read *don't walk on the plants,* but after a minilesson about how tone affects readers, she decided to go with a more positive directive rather than leave readers wondering just where they could walk.

Materials: For rough drafts, your sign makers can make use of whatever they use in any writing drafts. If you cut draft paper the size that you anticipate the final products will be, students will get a sense of how to set up the sign, how large to write, and how big to make the images. Banner paper works well for the *temporary* signs announcing special events; something more permanent like cardboard or even a scrap of wood could make a longer-lasting entry sign. Since color is key to the messages, provide crayons, markers, or whatever color mediums you have. Your signs will last longer if made of sturdy cardstock, and lamination will protect them from rain and snow. If they're outside, you'll want to check some of the guidelines for StoryWalks® on pages 39–41 in Chapter 3.

Interpretive Signage

Interpretive signs are the link between visitors and place. Effective panels invite readers to connect to the immediate surroundings—past and present—through engaging words and images. The authors of a classic resource in interpretation, *Signs, Trails, and Wayside Exhibits* (Gross, Zimmerman, and Buchholz 2006), write that a good sign should enrich the experience of the moment. The National Association of Interpretation (NAI) explains that *interpretive* work helps visitors make connections to place (Caputo, Lewis, and Brochu 2008). We can encounter interpretive signage in numerous settings, such as state and local parks, zoos, aquariums, nature centers, and museums and historical sites, among others. Successful interpretation offers an interesting message in minutes, and while it is a genre that is rarely taught, creating interpretive signs provides opportunities for students to develop as writers as they use short text, images, and awareness of audience to craft a powerful message. Your student writers can use the guidelines created by professional interpreters and graphic designers to share information in concise, engaging, and visual ways.

Writing interpretive signs

Freeman Tilden (2013), a leader in the field of interpretation, challenged designers to *provoke, reveal, and relate.* One way that this has played out in sign creation is a research-based trade mantra used by designers and writers of interpretive panels: the *3-30-3 rule* (Gross, Zimmerman, and Buchholz 2006). This means that as a writer, you've got *3 seconds* to grab a reader's attention and about *30 seconds* to convey your main idea. If you've succeeded in intriguing them, you then consider what further information and worthy details you can offer to someone who has *3 minutes* more to spend!

Here's a look at how the 3-30-3 rule might inform writing:

The *3-30-3 Rule* Used by Interpretive Designers

	What can I do in this time?	How might I do it?
3 seconds	• Grab the reader's attention • Intrigue them with a quick thought • Offer them something to take away	• Catchy title or headline (often a question or surprising fact) • Engaging photo or image • Large graphics
30 seconds	• Provide new knowledge	• Main message • Large lettering • 1–2 paragraphs
3 minutes	• Keep them digging deeper • Convince them it's worth 3 minutes of their time	• Keep it simple and vibrant • Smaller details and graphics

Figure 5-7   The 3-30-3 Rule

Reading nonfiction sets up student writers for creating interpretive panels

If you're like me, you are probably already thinking *that sounds a lot like nonfiction picture books*! In discussing my aha moment with nonfiction writer and advocate Melissa Stewart, she agreed that many of the strategies are similar, although called by different names. She noted that there are lots of expository picture book authors that *layer text* in much the same way as interpretive sign creators.

Here's how the 3-30-3 rule might look in nonfiction. Who can pass up a title, hook, or lede like: *What Do You Do with a Tail Like This?* (Jenkins and Page 2003), or *No Monkeys, No Chocolate* (Stewart and Young 2013)? Once you are hooked, the main ideas appear, followed by more detail in sidebars or in the back matter for readers whose curiosity is piqued or who are ready for more information. Stock your classroom library with expository nonfiction (as opposed to narrative nonfiction, which is more story-like in structure) and invite your students to note how the authors get our attention, tell us more, and then offer rich detail in a variety of ways. Lean on well-known and award-winning authors and illustrators like Steve Jenkins, Gail Gibbons, Melissa Stewart, and Jess Keating to help your readers notice how they do this: What is their 3-second hook? Is it the title? The headings? How do they present their 30-second chunk of information? Through their main ideas? What about for those readers who want even more information?

Similar Strategies Used by Interpretive Sign Designers and Nonfiction Picture Book Authors/Illustrators

	How we see this in Expository Nonfiction	How we see this in Interpretive Signs or Panels
3 seconds— grab readers' attention	Titles like: *Actual Size* (Jenkins) *Pink Is for Blobfish: Discovering the World's Perfectly Pink Animals* (Keating) *How to Swallow a Pig: Step-by-Step Advice from the Animal Kingdom* (Jenkins) *Can an Aardvark Bark?* (Stewart) *Elephants Can Paint Too!* (Arnold) Headings on a page, like: *How to defend yourself like an armadillo* *How to sew like a tailorbird* (From *How to Swallow a Pig*) *Can a seal squeal?* *Can a giraffe laugh?* (From *Can an Aardvark Bark?*)	Opening statements, like: *If you were standing here in 1959, you would be under water!* *Close your eyes and take a deep breath. What do you smell?* *Do you have what it takes to be a squirrel?*
30 seconds— give the main idea or gist	One to two short paragraphs, or one page per topic or idea, works well in the books above.	One to two paragraphs for the main idea is the goal.

continues

Similar Strategies Used by Interpretive Sign Designers and Nonfiction Picture Book Authors/Illustrators

	How we see this in Expository Nonfiction	How we see this in Interpretive Signs or Panels
3 minutes— offer details and deeper content	Many nonfiction writers use sidebars, bubbles, or panels along the bottom to offer more detail. You might also find these extensions in the back matter of the book. Gail Gibbons always has "fun facts," and Steve Jenkins usually presents a thumbnail summary about the animals found earlier in the book for curious readers.	These may be conveyed in an extra paragraph across the bottom, or in smaller paragraphs connected to the topic they are illuminating.

Figure 5-8　Connections between nonfiction picture books and interpretive signage

Head-heart-hand: How do professional designers approach their work?

Three graphic designer-interpretive planners met with me to share their approaches to creating powerful interpretive panels. Maja Smith, Sandra Murphy, and Jim Brangan have worked on interpretive panels including lake and history trails, museums, and even a fish hatchery and coffin factory. While all of them are guided by the 3-30-3 Rule, once they've researched the basic content for their panel, these interpreters also think about reaching their readers by addressing what they call the *head*, *heart*, and *hand*. After your students have collected or researched information to share, you might use this as a supportive frame for them as they consider the voice and tone of their interpretive sign. In planning their writing, encourage your students to ask themselves:

► Head: What facts about my topic are important to share? What information do I want to offer my readers?

► Heart: How do I want readers to feel after reading this? What emotions do I want to elicit from my readers?

► Hand: What can I ask readers to do as they read the sign right now, and what might they want to do later? For example, I might appeal to their senses. Do I want them to listen for birds? Touch a 3D model? As for later, how might I inspire them to recycle more? To find out more about my topic? This might help lead my reader to activism or to more learning!

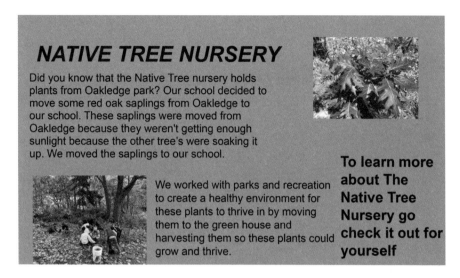

Figure 5-9 and Figure 5-10

Fifth graders culminated their unit on the native tree nursery and wildlife corridor by sharing key facts with the community. Their teacher asked them to consider how to present the content addressing *head, heart,* and *hand,* and to use the graphic elements of font, color, layout, and supporting images such as photographs, charts, or diagrams.

When Hilary Hamilton, a fifth- and sixth-grade teacher in Philadelphia, noticed that many residents of the neighborhood had lost their connection to the school when a new building went up, she began to plan a curricular unit to research the old building by inviting her students to interview alumni and neighbors; students would then present their work through interpretive panels that would honor the past. The content of the panels might include the facts of the old school's history for the *head,* the shared stories could touch the *heart,* and textual prompts to notice visual clues to the past—like the same street corner or flagpole— might represent the element of *hand,* or an action.

In Burlington, Vermont, Aziza Malik and her student teacher, Kayla Chaplin, worked with their fifth-grade class to create an animal travel corridor that would connect two small, wooded areas on either side of their school. The corridor would also support a native tree nursery. Students researched different types of animal crossings, created an action plan, and culminated their project through writing interpretive panels. Visitors to the corridor come

Figure 5-11   Interpretive panel at the Morris Arboretum, Philadelphia

away with a better understanding of the importance of the crossing (*head*), perhaps filled with happiness or relief for the animals and admiration for the students' efforts (*heart*), and interest in knowing more about other types of animal crossings (*hand*, or *action*).

A close look at one interpretive sign

Immersing students in the genre of interpretive signage will allow them to notice and apply their ideas of what an effective sign is like. Beyond annoyance at their efforts to hijack my birdfeeders, I have never taken the time to appreciate squirrels until I took a look at this sign at the Morris Arboretum (Figure 5–11). I had a lot of ground to cover during my visit, but could not pass by the question *Do* you *have what it takes to be a* squirrel? Whoever created this sign nailed the 3-second rule; I was hooked! In just 30 seconds, I walked away with a new appreciation for squirrels; moving forward, I will admire their strength and balance as I shoo them away from my birdfeeders. Figure 5–12 invites us to think about how we could discuss the *head/heart/hand* framework with young interpretive writers.

A starting list of minilessons for creating signage

Just as in any writing workshop, you'll want to create minilessons to help your students tackle this new genre. All of these are strategies that professional interpreters use to make their text direct and compelling, and your students can, too. These might include:

▶ Writing in the second person. *I'm talking to you.* Many effective interpretive signs are written in the second person, or addressing *you*, to connect the reader to the space. Note how the header on the squirrel poster in Figure 5–11 addresses the reader directly: *Do* you *have what it takes to be a squirrel?* It's easy to imagine that readers will be eager to find out! There are numerous nonfiction picture book examples to share with your students to help them hear how this sounds. For example, in Molly Bang and Penny Chisolm's *Buried Sunlight: How Fossil Fuels Have*

Reaching Your Readers by Addressing Their *Head*, *Heart*, and *Hand*

Include something for your readers'	How will you engage them at these levels?	How you might write it	How do these appear in the squirrel panel?
Head	What do you want your reader to know when they're done reading this?	What is the one main idea? What are some details or examples to share that help them understand?	Squirrels have balance, grip, keen senses, and strength.
Heart	What do you want them to feel while they are reading?	What is a surprising or startling fact that will touch their feelings?	Wow! Squirrels are amazing! I feel impressed—and maybe surprised— about their strength.
Hand	What do you want them to do while reading? Many of us remember something better when we are active.	Invite them to use their senses: close their eyes and listen, look in a certain direction, touch a raised map. Offer them a next step or action: where to find out more information? Where to visit next?	This panel invites me to go try out a human-sized net to see the woods from a squirrel's perspective.

Figure 5-12   How can we see *head*, *heart*, *hand* in the squirrel sign?

Changed the Earth (2014), the author makes the complex topic of energy more accessible by having the sun narrate the book, addressing the reader as *you*. In *How to Swallow a Pig: Step-by-Step Advice from the Animal Kingdom,* Steve Jenkins (2015) gives the readers step-by-step directives such as "Chop down some trees," and "Complete your dam" in a way that is completely engaging and has readers ready to go out and crack a nut like a crow or spin a web like a spider.

▶ Tone. All the professional interpreters I interviewed gave me the same message. *While addressing head, heart, and hand, use accurate language, but imagine you are writing to inform a friend or your favorite relative.* In other words, use words that you are familiar with and write directly to that person. Not only will you use words that come naturally to you, but you will already have established a way of communicating that feels comfortable. Turn and talk sessions would be a good way to rehearse this type of writing once students know the content of what they want to convey.

▶ Use short sentences. Since interpretive signage is often read on the go, or as part of a bigger experience—think hike, museum, or history exhibit—your reader is not settling in for a long read. Your message can be brief; save more complex constructions for other genres.

▶ Specific words get the message across. While the sentences may be short, the words matter. This is where new knowledge about their topic or site will empower your writers. Instead of *the side of the hill changed over time*, here's the place to use their new science word, *erode*. *Erode* is a more precise word, explaining just *how* the hill changed, and has the added benefit of keeping the text on the short side. Instead of *Use all your senses to touch, listen, see, and smell*, be direct and invite action. *Close your eyes. Take a deep breath. Touch the rough edge of the stone.* All these strategies will tighten the connection between the reader and writer.

▶ Experiment with different platforms for designing a panel. Digital formats such as Google Slides, Book Creator, and Adobe Express Page can provide templates for design. One-pagers offers the same opportunity for drafting in a hands-on format. Using one page replicates one panel, and your writers can get a better sense of how each part will fit together. Another approach might be to have them compose on large index cards that they place on poster board.

Set Up a Structure for Your Future Interpreters

Since student populations naturally change completely every few years as they grow and move on, it makes sense that interpretive signage in your setting will change, too. Some curricular units repeat, and new classes may want to update information. New murals, outdoor features, and indoor exhibits will undoubtedly morph as we learn more about various topics and have better access to materials. For that reason, just like the StoryWalk® structures, you'll want to make structures that can last for a while but allow for panels to be changed by new student populations.

The power and potential of writing interpretive signs

Interpretive panels help readers connect to a place, event, or feature, and are a great way for students to represent knowledge with an authentic setting. What do the third graders in their garden, the Philadelphia students in their neighborhood, and the fifth graders creating an animal passage have in common? All are immersed in a place-based curriculum project that a broader audience can learn from through interpretive signage. Each of these examples emerged from a concern or interest that mattered to the students and connected to the school curriculum. Students learned to create

Figure 5-13 Tweaking letters invites readers to look up or around.

a message to help readers both understand the importance of the project and discover their own connection to an event or place.

Special features of a school or park are another element worthy of interpretive signage. To invite readers to look up, students might add playful arrows to letters, directing eyes upward or inviting viewers to go around a corner.

Signage explaining the backstory of a powerful mural on the street side of a city elementary school offers any passerby the chance to understand its meaning and to discover their own connection to the mural long after its unveiling ceremonies.

The power of interpretive signage is that it can enrich a visitor's experience even if no one else is around. And this is the exciting challenge for the interpreter—to craft writing that informs, touches, and engages the reader's head, heart, and hand.

Signs of Expression

While many signs help us connect to a place or event, signs can also be used to express opinions and feelings. These signs represent our strong feelings with short and powerful word choices, and we expect to see them at protests, sports events, and polling places. Many rely on the same *head, heart, hand* guidelines that shape interpretive signs. Sign makers clearly want to attract attention quickly and invite viewers to feel and think about whatever issue or event is at hand. Depending on your curriculum or events at your school, your students might want to create signs like these that invite them to express their thoughts, opinions, and feelings in just a few words and images:

- **Signs for a cause:** People make signs for public display that express concerns about issues and problems that matter to them. Protest signs have a long history in a country that values free speech; students learning about climate change, events in history, human rights, and other issues important to them may be interested in this form of public expression. Fifth

continues

continued from previous page

graders successfully lobbied the Vermont state legislature to make snowboarding the state sport using signs they created to get their message across. Many communities across the country are creating pollinator habitats, and signs urging neighbors to *Save the Bees!* are common.

- **Voting Signs:** During a federal, state, or local election year, yard and rally signs pop up everywhere with candidate names and issues presented in short text with carefully chosen colors and memorable logos and slogans. These may provide models for your students as they vote in school or classroom elections or try to influence each other in making decisions for their school community. Learning about how to use graphic design and symbols in their own signs will help students develop into more savvy readers of such signage in their own lives.

- **Supportive Signs:** Go Team! Whether on a school or community sports or academic team, signs are visual ways to support players. Spelling bee champs—whether they win or lose the district spell-off—would feel supported by a sign like *G-R-E-A-T job!* We often see congratulatory and sympathetic wishes, as well as cheers of recognition on signs from digital displays to banners at the entrance to schools. Giving students agency in these public-facing messages is an authentic use of literacy and requires them to think carefully about how to convey important ideas and feelings in just a few words.

- **Bumper Stickers:** Upon moving to Burlington, my family couldn't help but wonder about the story behind the ubiquitous sticker *Keep Vermont Weird*. While they aren't drivers yet, elementary students can take note of bumper stickers, one of the most compressed ways of expressing an idea. You might challenge your students to apply what they've learned about their own city, town, or state by creating a bumper sticker phrase that represents a key characteristic like another common one around here: *Vermont— Green Mountain State*.

Figure 5-14 This sign expresses school community feeling.

Inspiration in children's books

There is a small but growing selection of children's books that can help students see the power of signs to convey opinions. You will want to provide some context about events in the books so that your students can appreciate both the relationship between the significant events and the power of the signs.

The Bobbin Girl (Emily Arnold McCully)

Brave Girl: Clara and the Shirtwaist Makers' Strike of 1909 (Michelle Markel)

Let the Children March (Monica Clark-Robinson)

Our House Is on Fire: Greta Thunberg's Call to Save the Planet (Jeanette Winter)

Vote! (Eileen Christelow)

If I Ran for President (Catherine Stier)

Click, Clack, Moo: Cows That Type (Doreen Cronin)

Resources

Cascade Interpretive Consulting. 2004. *Interpretive and Wayfinding Plan: Washington Park Arboretum.* Seattle: Lehrman Cameron Studio.

Gross, Michael, Ronald Zimmerman, and Jim Buchholz. 2006. *Signs, Trails, and Wayside Exhibits: Connecting People and Places*. 3rd ed. Stevens Point, WI: University of Wisconsin-Stevens Point Foundation Press.

Tilden, Freeman. 2008. *Interpreting Our Heritage.* Durham, NC: The University of North Carolina Press.

McGregor, Tanny. 2018. *Ink & Ideas: Sketchnotes for Engagement, Comprehension, and Thinking.* Portsmouth, NH: Heinemann.

Moline, Steve. 1995. *I See What You Mean: Children at Work with Visual Information*. Portland, ME: Stenhouse.

———. 2011. *I See What You Mean: Visual Literacy K–8*. 2nd ed. Portsmouth, NH: Stenhouse.

6

LITERACY TRAILS

Trails Take Us Somewhere New

Trails motivate us to see what's just up ahead, or around the corner. Even in literature, from the trail of crumbs that Hansel and Gretel create, to the classic yellow brick road and Shel Silverstein's *Where the Sidewalk Ends,* trails hint at adventure and reward us with new sensory experiences, surprises, and a chance to explore our surroundings as we go. A project called *#chalkyourwalk,* initiated during the pandemic, led to communities chalking temporary but powerful messages and art along trails in urban and suburban areas. The New York City Public Library has inspirational quotations about reading, writing, and literature embedded in the sidewalk along East Forty-first Street, aka *Library Way.* In Charlottetown, the capital of Prince Edward Island, children hunt downtown for nine miniature mouse sculptures—characters that make a beloved island story come alive.

A trail may invite you to go in a new direction, although even traveling a familiar path or a loop means that you may come back to the start a little bit changed. Jack, a main character in Sondheim's musical *Into the Woods* (1999), reflects on his adventure up the beanstalk and notices that he's different upon his return than before his climb. Using your senses to observe your surroundings, completing challenges, and experiencing the enjoyment of being outside can enable us to come back a little different, to view the world differently. And literacy can play a role in this transformation.

Which Path to Take?

Like the other approaches offered in this book, there are many ways into creating a literacy trail depending on your setting, from spontaneous chalking of sensory trails to a concerted school community-wide initiative to create permanent walking trails. For simplicity's sake, I've divided these into two main categories. You might use Trails of Application and Practice for reviewing, applying, and practicing new skills and strategies. Trails of Connection and Exploration invite you to use some of the approaches from earlier chapters to share information with an audience about a themed trail. You and your students will quickly realize that, like any categories, these models are open to hybridization, and you'll find your own ways to create the best *trail mix* that works for you.

Trails of application and practice

Design a trail for the application or practice of new ideas or skills. Like some of the learning experiences in Chapter 2, the *Literacy to Go* chapter, your trails of application and practice can be as simple as moving indoor classroom activities outdoors onto an asphalt play area, sidewalk, or existing pathway. For these, you'll want a surface that can be drawn on. Choose or sketch out an existing path or design one that is linear, serpentine, or a loop. With your bucket of chalk and blacktop area or path, invite your students to apply and practice some of their literacy learning. You'll quickly figure out the range of possibilities, but here are a few—sensory trails, curricular paths, concept paths, word pattern paths, and book trails—to try as you launch your own.

Sensory trails

Long a staple for physical and occupational therapists, sensory trails focused on movement have been popping up in school hallways as ways for students to focus energy and interpret sensory symbols. The pandemic saw these rise in popularity as physical education and classroom teachers filmed themselves and their families having fun on the driveway or sidewalk and shared these with their virtual classes. Essentially, participants follow a series of symbols that indicate movements requiring concentration, balance, and controlled movement, as suggested in Figure 6–1. You can create contrasting moves involving quick action with slow breathing, interspersed with balance challenges. You'll want to be sure that students can find their own way in, so allow for various interpretations of the symbols. A student on crutches and one in a wheelchair may interpret the spiral spin symbol uniquely. Once your students have experienced a few of these, challenge them to come up with their own symbols for various moves.

While sensory trails typically focus on movement, their very name hints at our senses. Brainstorm with your class about how you might include touch, smell, sight, and sound. Include an eye, ear, or nose symbol to indicate a pause to notice what's around using these senses. A hand could invite participants to feel the texture of the trail or plants around it. If it's snack time, incorporate that into the trail to satisfy their sense of taste. A quick search on the internet for *sensory trails* will provide you lots of examples, but the ones below and in Figure 6–2 can get you started:

Symbols for Creating a Sensory Trail

Symbols	Movement—students can individualize what each symbol means for them.	How might your students have fun with drawing the movement once they're familiar with the moves?
◎◎	Spin (with reverse direction)	Tornado Snail Windmill Anything with a spiral!
▬ ▐▐	Jump (direction of lines could indicate that the jumper turns)	Branches Skis Popsicle sticks
○○○○	Hop	Lily pads Launch pads Boulders
WWW WWW ～	Balance-walk along a zigzag, serpentine, or loopy line	Rivers Snakes Wind Snail trails
〰	Take deep breaths	Balloons Wind Sniffing Nose

Figure 6-1

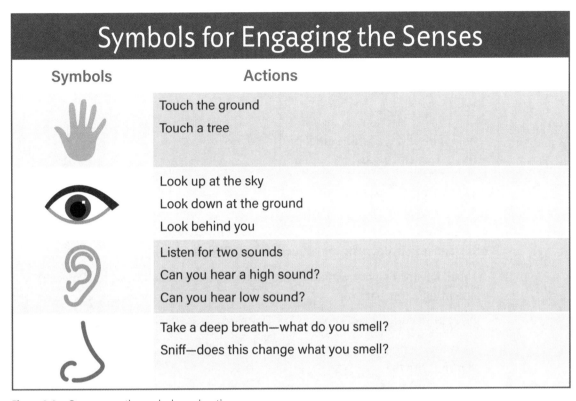

Figure 6-2 Sensory path symbols and actions

Curricular paths

Whatever ideas you want your learners to engage with inside, there's probably a way to bring them outside. The possibilities are endless. Hopping, jumping, gliding, and moving may not only motivate students to practice patterns, apply concepts, and define vocabulary, but the repetition motivated by physical activity may mean that they actually get more practice and have a lot of fun doing it. They'll also internalize the idea that thinking about learning isn't just for indoors! Here are some examples of how you can take learning out for a spin on a path of practice or application.

A word pattern jump or roll based on the root or rime *ick* could look like this:

ick jump or roll

ick

pick

lick

nick

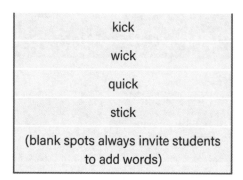

kick
wick
quick
stick
(blank spots always invite students to add words)

Figure 6-3

More ideas and tweaks for individualized challenges

► Label only the first box with the word pattern; jumpers chalk in words for each other that fit the pattern.

► Provide an onset of one or two letters and let jumpers fill in relevant rhymes.

► You provide **th**; jumpers might add: **an, en, ink, ing**, and so on to create words starting with **th**.

► Root words with suffixes and/or prefixes. You provide **box**; jumpers add **er, ed, ing**.

► Synonyms. You provide **blue**; jumpers add **teal, turquoise, azure, royal, navy, sky, periwinkle**.

Concept paths

You might use the same or a similar template to review your science curriculum by creating a concept jump or roll like the ones below about *living things* or the *water cycle*:

Jump or roll to the LIVING things	
Flower	Swing
Stapler	Bird
Pencil	Elephant
Worm	Tree

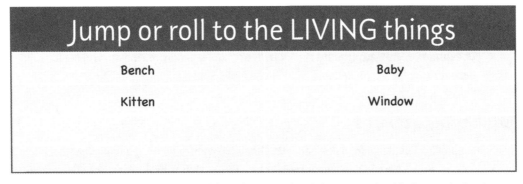

Jump or roll to the LIVING things

Bench	Baby
Kitten	Window

Figure 6-4 Students can add words to this task or populate it from scratch with the words they've been learning. You'll want to set up enough grids so that everyone is engaged.

Water Cycle	Drawing, example, or definition
Evaporate	
Cloud	
Rain	
Droplet	
Vapor	
Precipitation	
Snow	
Cycle	
Land	

Figure 6-5 Water cycle vocabulary: hop or roll to each word and provide a drawing, example, or definition.

Many curricular areas can follow a path

Once you've done a few of these, you'll see that you can plug in concepts and terms from other curricular areas. Some common ones might include:

► Names: at the beginning of the year, add every classmate's name and practice reading and calling them out as you jump, roll, or hop

► Planet names: written, drawn, or both

► Sneaking this into a literacy book: counting and other math facts, like multiples of twos or fives, simple sums, or fractions

► Vocabulary for any unit; land on a word, articulate a definition (or land on a definition, give the term), or draw an example.

Book trails or paths

While Chapter 3 provides a focus on StoryWalks®, an experience with a complete book, why not engage your learners in *creating* a path that will get them thinking about a book? Here are several ways this could go:

► **Make a trail for book retelling or sharing.** If you ask your students to do retellings, challenge them to retell the story on a path.

• For younger students, this could mean that as you elicit a retelling from the group, they can each draw their own interpretation of that element along the path.

• Once this becomes a familiar response to a book, you might follow your read-aloud or book discussion by assigning partners to different parts of the path, with some students tackling the beginning, others the middle, and of course, the end. Help them use their trail lingo and ask that the *lead* draws or writes about the beginning, the *pack* shares about the middle, and the *sweep* reveals the ending.

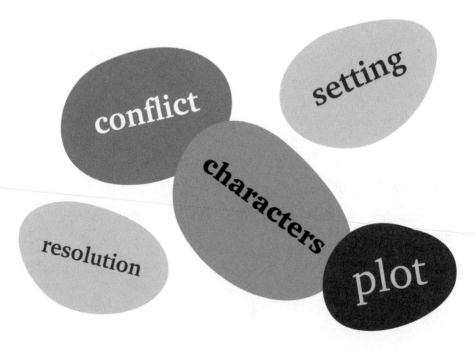

Figure 6-6
Use stones or signs with literary elements to prompt chalk responses from readers about their current books. Nonfiction could include *type of nonfiction, interesting facts, text features.*

- If your goals include discussion of conventional story elements like *characters*, *setting*, *problem*, *solution*, and *surprises*, a word stone or sign—posted as in a StoryWalk®—could prompt them for their response to each of these literary elements.
- For older students, once they've got the hang of retelling a story on a path, you might provide them with a template to carry on their clipboards that prompts them to address genre, writing style, characters, setting, plot, problem, and resolution along different sections of the path. You might brainstorm with them ahead of time. Jot some chalk notes near their starting point for them to refer to. They might retell the story using words or images—or a combination.

▶ **Create a path as a hook to intrigue readers.** Think about who would like this book and how to promote it to other readers. Challenge readers to give just enough information to intrigue. This could be a great way to start a book swap day; with the right weather and enough books or a resourceful librarian, you could place the book at the end of the trail, ready for the now eager reader.

▶ **Book trails can be for all ages.** Younger children might enjoy recreating colorful food items that tempt *The Very Hungry Caterpillar* (Carle). Having them each choose one to draw along a path would emphasize just how much this creature ate. Older students might consider books that would be more challenging to chalk; how might you convey the main ideas in a longer book like *Charlotte's Web* (White), *Front Desk* (Yang), or *All Thirteen: The Incredible Cave Rescue of the Thai Boys' Soccer Team* (Soontornvat)? It makes sense here to create a book trail based on a class read-aloud, with everyone contributing ideas for sections of the book to be represented on different parts of the trail. Once they've got the hang of it, you could invite pairs and small groups to create book trails based on literature circle books. Creating a path representation of a book invites dipping back into the book to confirm and reference key elements.

▶ **Trail styles can reflect the type of text.** The idea of a book path could work for many types of writing, too. Explore how different genres might be represented differently on a trail. For example, it's easy to imagine a story unfolding through twists and turns along a path created by an individual writer or pairs. What might a cliff-hanger look like? What form might a story in free verse take? How might chapters shape the trail? Might you use a different color chalk for each? Create a thicker border between chapters? Layered nonfiction offers the challenge of how to include bold text, sidebars, and other possibilities for trail offshoots.

Create your own trail mix!

Once students are familiar with these paths of practice and application, mix it up. You might choose symbols from the sensory trails to enhance or emphasize aspects of their trails. For

The Day the Crayons Quit by Drew Daywalt	
Characters	Duncan, the artist The crayons
Setting	Classroom
Problem	Duncan's crayons complain that they are always used to draw the same thing
Solution	Duncan uses the colors differently in a new drawing. Red sun, green water, yellow sky
Surprises	It made me think about my own drawings

Figure 6-7   Use stones or signs in Figure 6–6 to prompt your readers to respond to a book they have read.

example, students might want to invite their participants to *take a deep* breath midway through a story path or do a spin or two to break up word study work. Ask them to think about how a meandering line could emphasize the meandering of a story; jumping and rolling from fact to fact in a display of nonfiction could emphasize a list of facts.

Trails of connection and exploration

Whether on a sidewalk, a trail through the woods, or a dirt path, trails invite us to connect to nature and outdoors in general. We hear sounds generated by birds and insects, we feel shade, breezes, and temperature changes, and we make discoveries about nature; for example, within the category of *trees* are many smaller categories, including different leaf shapes, shades of green, and canopy shapes. Inviting students to notice what's around them and to reflect on and interpret what they are observing helps to develop their awareness and provides them with firsthand experiences to talk, write, and draw about. Your setting may accommodate trails on your own grounds, in adjacent parks, or in neighborhoods.

If you are ambitious, partnerships with local parks, recreation, and conservation organizations can open possibilities for using existing trails. These partners may also be able to provide you with support and guidance in creating your own trails in your own setting, if you have the opportunity to start from scratch. A partnership could range from a one-time guest speaking engagement to a year-long commitment or residency. Regardless of the scope of your trails, and whether you are using existing trails or creating your own, you and your class will be captivated by learning from those experienced in trailblazing.

Most likely, you will be working with trails that already exist, and you can think of these as the *hardware*, or the length, direction, and surface of the trail you will be using. Once you're familiar with this trail, you're ready to think about the *software*—the trail name, the ways that trails can invite and inspire literacy experiences and personal connections to a trail. Julia Robertson, author of *Dirty Teaching: A Beginner's Guide to Learning Outdoors*, notes that children love to make trails and treasure hunts. She observes that not only does trail-making invite students to learn about a natural space or local area, but it also engages them with figuring out how to give and follow directions and order and sequence events (2014, 168).

Make your first move

Whatever your setting, you will find nature outside, ranging from birds and clouds to pollinators and woods. Inviting students to connect with nature on a trail or sidewalk offers them a chance to use their senses to connect, explore, and gather firsthand observations. You might take a first walk and then list all the observations on a communal chart upon your return to your classroom. Subsequent trips could involve

Walk an Inch in Their Shoes: Playing with Scale

Life-size trails are great, but if you have limited space, or you want to offer your students something new, challenge them to create a practice path or book trail in miniature! The popularity of Lego worlds and fairy houses attest to the appeal of the tiny. Students could move pebble markers along miniature word study paths or create a *meeple** as their traveler on a minibook or sensory trail (*meeple=a small figure used as a playing piece in a game).

Figure 6-8   Meeples can represent characters in books. Students would enjoy making their own.

In his book, *Childhood and Nature: Design Principles for Education,* one of David Sobel's principles addresses *small worlds.* He believes that when children create miniature representations, they work at developing a bigger picture or understanding. Just as dollhouses and block play invite understandings of the bigger world, in some ways miniature trails and paths can serve as models for larger ones. They can also serve as drafts for drawing and writing. And we know that they appeal to small children and small fingers!

clipboards, science journals, or writing notebooks for expanding on these observations. You might include prompts like:

- What do you see? Hear? Smell? Touch?
- What changes do you notice since our last visit?
- What questions do you have?

Another form of prompts could be a deck of cards with a specific question or suggestion on each. A nature card game, Aqua Marooned!, described below, is a perfect example of inclusive cards that invite trail walkers to connect their own lived experience with nature to being outdoors anywhere. Teachers could create a few of these cards and then invite students to expand the deck of possibilities.

Aqua Marooned! A Card Game to Help You Interact with Nature

Adrienne Mackey, a theatre artist and professor of theatre, created a card game designed to play anywhere and get people outside. The cards in the deck are inclusive, building on people's own experiences with nature. While the cards are somewhat generic, allowing players to use them anywhere outdoors, there are also expansion packs that relate to specific sites.

Figures 6-9, 6-10, and 6-11
These examples invite players to listen, watch, and create.

While the original game design is framed as aliens visiting earth, and players compete for points, you and your students can create interactive cards that participants use for their own purposes. Aqua Marooned! provides guidelines for creating your own cards, found below:

* *Vary the activity to suit different players' interests and strengths.* When creating cards for the game, it's important to design a variety of activities so the game supports all players. Some cards in the deck include closing your eyes and listening for sounds, spotting birds, or naming pond dwellers.

* *Avoid yes-or-no questions.* Your goal is to stimulate discussion, so cards should form questions in a way that opens them up for dialogue and avoids one simple "right" response. Asking, "Have you ever saved an animal?" invites a yes-or-no answer; asking players to tell about a time they might have helped an animal supports narrative development and may serve as a prewriting experience.

* *Be inclusive of nature newbies.* A key goal for Aqua Marooned! was to create a game that would be as fun to play if you're visiting nature for the very first time or have years of environmental experience under your belt. Cards that encourage observation and creative interpretation of present surroundings allow first-timers to feel as prepared as anyone else to play.

* *Find personal connections.* Everyone is an expert when speaking to their unique lived experience. Frame questions on cards in a way that invites players to talk about their lives and feelings. "Why does nature matter to you?" is an example of a question that lets players bring their subjective experience to the game.

* *Zoom out!* Just as the interpretive signage mantra aims to inspire readers to act and think beyond their immediate experience, the creators of Aqua Marooned! hope to awaken curiosity in players and to apply what they have thought about in the game to their lived lives.

Creating themed trails to connect learning and place

A fourth-grade teacher shared that on a field trip to the Lowell textile mills, a history trail through the buildings enabled her students to connect with historical events that had taken place in those very spots. A trek through recent snow on their playground in Iowa allowed kindergarteners to notice and identify animal tracks. Precisely because they are situated in a specific place, trails can connect us to historical events, special events, and features of where we live and go to school. They help us relate our own experiences to our surroundings. By no means exhaustive, Figure 6–12 on the next page can get you started thinking about ways you might use a trail to connect with local history or key people, landmarks, and neighborhoods.

A Sampler of Trails You Might Create with Your Class

Trail themes	Examples	Invite your students to
Historical events	• Freedom Trail in Boston • Lowell Textile Mills • Baltimore National Heritage Trail • San Antonio Missions Trail	Create a trail to culminate a unit from your local history curriculum.
Unique people and features	Famous people in your setting such as: • athletes • artists • politicians • inventors Famous place features: • a factory • a landmark (cliff, river, lake) • an interesting building	Research a famous local personality and create a biographical trail. Study a local feature and interpret it for others: • What makes it special?
Literature trails	Feature books written and/or illustrated by local authors and illustrators	After an author/illustrator study, create a biographical trail of a local illustrator or author, and feature information about their signature techniques. Invite them to take the trail!
Nature trails	Feature: • trees • plants • rocks & boulders • birds • insects	Design brochures, identification signs, or guided tours or podcasts to share knowledge about natural features along a nature trail.
Neighborhood trails	*City Trails: New York* (Lonely Planet for Kids) offers up trails based on themes like *trash*, *food*, *transportation*, *Halloween*, and *local treasures.* Your setting may allow you to create a neighborhood or downtown trail based on a theme.	Design a trail based on curricular units about community, nutrition and food, transportation, or government.

Pick one theme or topic and create a trail sharing information, using identification signs and the *3-30-3* or *head, heart, hand* guidelines shared in Chapter 5.

Figure 6–12

Trails invite literacy involvement

Whether your trail is in a nearby park or on your own grounds, implicit in the idea of a trail is that others will take it too. This provides a perfect opportunity to consider audience (see Figure 6–14). Invite your students to address potential audiences for your trail. Ask them who will be taking the trail and what will they want to know? What will enhance their experience? Take the trail a few times with notebooks in hand and ask them to use their senses to observe special features of the trail, such as a unique tree, or a sharp turn, scents, and other notable elements. Which of these do they want to share with other trail users? Approaches described in earlier chapters, such as signage, StoryWalks®, and using word stones as trail markers, can be employed in establishing and sharing characteristics of a trail. Start with an approach that matches your curricular goals and layer on others as you individualize the experience and as students become increasingly experienced and confident.

Trail lingo

It's always fun to be a language insider, and trails have their own special terms. These terms (Figure 6–15 on pages 105–106) help convey what is unique and important about trails, and even how we use them in other ways, *off-trail.* Share these with your students and then generate some new ones together.

Using Trails to Discover the Hidden

Our senses inform us pretty well; my scientist friend tells me that we use them as tools to understand our environment all the time. Some of us might hear a bird's song and feel the sun's warmth ushering in a new season. But what about things we can't see or hear or notice in some way with our senses? A common science topic for elementary students is plants, and the photo below offers an ingenious way for us to understand the deep root system of a tree. An urban school's trail might represent a subway system below a path. Work with your local departments of public works, conservation, and transportation to see what you might represent on your paths. Help your students better understand natural and engineered systems that may not be obvious to us using our senses.

Figure 6-13   Painted tree roots offer visitors a visual sense of the breadth of this tree's root system. Morris Arboretum, University of Pennsylvania.

Ways to Reach an Audience on a Trail

Approach	Why choose this approach?	Materials
Signage	Authentic use of voice; writing for an audience; use of the *3-30-3 Rule*	Laminated and mounted information about the trail or specific elements along the trail
Personal Guide	Oral communication of gathered information in an engaging way, live	Student-generated observations about the trail organized to share at relevant points
Brochures or Leaflets	Written communication using verbal (words) and visual (image) text	Information conveyed solely in writing for those exploring the trail on their own
Trail Markers	Use of maps, symbols, and relevant keys	Environmentally friendly paint for *blazes*, or trail markers made of wood or stone
QR Codes	Way to publish pieces about the trail	Free QR code software; finished student-written pieces are the landing site
Podcasts	Oral communication of gathered information in an engaging way, recorded. Could be a good "final draft" of the personal guide experience.	Recording devices and a site for sharing them

Figure 6-14   Invite your students to choose the way they want to convey information to trail walkers depending on their goals.

Fun with Trail Lingo

Term or Expression	What might it mean? What's it all about?
Trail head	Where a trail begins (and may end if it's a loop); at a trail head you might find: a geographical marker or a trail name, maps, a bench, brochures, and a key to blazes.
Trail off	To start strong and then slowly cease. Sometimes we do this with our voices. What might it mean for a trail?
Hit the trail	An expression meaning let's get started!
Trailblaze	Create the trail! Blaze the way. In some cases, *blazes*—or a swipe of paint color—are used interchangeably with trail markers.
Trail markers	A marker showing you the way to go on the trail. These may be painted on trees (with tree-friendly paint), small arrows, or signs.
Trail mix	Do snacks come to mind instantly? Give in to it; an outdoor snack can be a pleasure. Invite your students to think about other ways to interpret this phrase. How might you mix a sensory trail with a word study trail?
Off-trail	Made famous by adventurous skiers, going off-trail may offer ways of exploring "off the beaten path." Conversely, this phrase may help you establish where it's OK to walk—or not.
Lead	Much like a traditional class line leader, the lead should be aware of the group following, and set places to stop, gather, and be aware of the goal of the walk or hike.

continues

Fun with Trail Lingo

Term or Expression	What might it mean? What's it all about?
Sweep	The sweep brings up the end of the line, noting any dropped materials, provides support for peers, and is ready to alert the group should the pacing need to change. Communicates with the lead.
Leave no trace	A universally known guideline to leave nature undisturbed when you are trail walking or hiking. Pertains to everyone! A norm to be introduced and discussed. Some trail settings may call for a different ethos, if your purpose is to clean a trail or do a recycle sweep of the area.
Trail names	Trails may have enticing names that tell us about them: The Meander Trail, The Beeline, The Loop. What will you name your trail? Why?

Figure 6–15   Special settings evoke specific language. Play around with trail expressions and use a concept map to launch a discussion about other word groups. Some examples to get you going might include *sky*, *water*, and *dog*.

A starting list of books with trails

Hansel and Gretel (The Brothers Grimm)

The Hike (Alison Farrell)

Home in the Woods (Eliza Wheeler)

Journey (Aaron Becker)

Tiny, Perfect Things (M. H. Clark)

Where the Sidewalk Ends (Shel Silverstein)

The Wizard of Oz (L. Frank Baum)

Wonder Walkers (Micha Archer)

Resources

Robertson, Juliet. 2014. *Dirty Teaching: A Beginner's Guide to Learning Outdoors*. Carmarthen, Wales, UK: Independent Thinking Press.

Sobel, David. 2008. *Childhood and Nature: Design Principles for Education*. Portland, ME: Stenhouse.

Aqua Marooned! is a game that explores nature using quick wit, physical activity, and creative invention. Designed specifically for the Delaware River Watershed with guidance from the Nanticoke Lenni-Lenape Tribal Nation, many of the sites are in Philadelphia itself. Almost all the cards can be used anywhere in nature. This interactive card game playfully invites its participants to define, learn, and examine their surroundings.

MAKE IT HAPPEN

Strategies and Resources to Help You Move Literacy Outdoors

Figure 7-1

Inspired and Ready to Get Started?

Remember, there are lots of ways to move literacy outdoors depending on your setting, opportunities, and energy. One third-grade teacher observed: "At its best, moving literacy outside can involve meaningful integration with nature and place, but at the very least, just bringing a book outside—that's amazing! You can't go wrong." Whatever you are ready for, here is a quick-start list of possible strategies and resources to help you launch your efforts.

Administrative support

Administrators who understand your goals can be your biggest allies. Before meeting with your principal, consider which curricular and social goals moving outside will help your students achieve. These might include:

Figure 7-2

- ▶ Literacy goals such as practicing skills (word gardens, paths)

- ▶ Writing for an audience (Story-Walks®, signage)

- ▶ Exploring genres (poetry based on senses, signage, StoryWalks®)

- ▶ Independent reading and read-alouds to develop stamina and support enjoyment (themed backpacks)

- ▶ Social goals of partnerships in designing and completing tasks

- ▶ Applying concepts of literacy beyond the classroom.

In addition to your literacy goals, you may find that your administrator has some suggestions as well as ways to connect with other school initiatives. One special educator shared that her principal pointed her to a dedicated state grant for special educators to use in their curriculum.

Funding and potential donors

We often face limited budgets for materials. Teachers have reached out successfully to school- and community-based sources to support their outdoor literacy goals. You'll want to be sure that possible donors are aware of the connections to literacy and outdoor learning. Here are some teacher tried-and-true suggestions; approaching several sources might get you closer to what you need or want. Be sure to include how many students will be included, and that some of the funding will go to the materials and *hardware* that will support

Figure 7-3

many years of literacy experiences. They might want your assurance that their donations will be acknowledged in some way, and of course, writing thank-you notes serves several literacy goals.

- ▶ Local hardware and lumber stores

- ▶ Chain hardware and lumber stores

- ▶ Programs like DonorsChoose, GoFundMe, or other school-approved fundraising programs

- ▶ Parent-teacher organizations or associations

- ▶ Partner with a technical high school; one school built the structures for Story-Walks®, another built a wooden shed to store supplies

- ▶ Search online for grants from organizations like KidsGardening, Green School-yards America, and others supporting outdoor and nature learning. You may also find that literacy organizations will be interested in supporting your outdoor moves.

Partnerships

Figure 7-4

Many teachers have formed partnerships with local organizations and businesses:

- ▶ City and town departments of parks and recreation have experience with children interacting with the outdoors and with creating and maintaining trails. They are often interested in connecting with school populations.

► Conservation groups and departments and nature centers often have a goal of developing conservation awareness in young citizens. Together, you might create a project that will serve both your goals and theirs.

  • One conservation group in Traverse City, Michigan, partnered with students to create signage to inform and help protect a watershed.
  • A conservation group in rural Vermont partnered with a local library to sponsor seasonal story hikes.
  • A conservation group in a small city worked with elementary students to develop a tree nursery on the school grounds; the students wrote letters reaching out to possible eventual recipients of the saplings.

► Museums and historical societies

  • Many museums adapted their exhibits for outdoor display during the recent pandemic. Whether indoors or out, museums offer strong models of interpretive signage. A curator may be tapped as an expert for your signage designers.

► Libraries

  • Many libraries partner with schools already; librarians may visit classes to promote summer reading programs or notify students about ongoing story hours, reading clubs, and new books. Librarians are all about developing literacy stamina and habits in school populations and beyond.
  • When a library was closed during the pandemic, a wall of windows offered passersby a story experience; pages of a picture book were posted for a walk-along read. Your class might create an illustrated story or work of nonfiction for such a display at a partnering library.
  • Many libraries are developing a bank of StoryWalk® titles for loan; explore these to see whether any of them would appeal to your class and meet your curricular needs.

► Stores and other businesses

  • In addition to considering a request for donated materials (think paper, cardstock, paint, and other tools you'll need for culminating work), ask about how these partners use literacy in their settings and what expert advice they might share. What might they have to offer your students in terms of signage design? How do they attract attention? Convey information to a busy reader?

- Could this business be a site for a StoryWalk®? Fifth graders loved their own idea about posting a Lois Ehlert book, *Growing Vegetable Soup,* on display in the produce section of a local store. They also were eager to talk with airport officials about books on the walls for those waiting for their flights to be called at their gate.
- Brainstorm with your students about local settings they visit and what would be authentic and entertaining reading. Depending on your students' age, you might either challenge them to write a proposal to a specific business or tackle this communication yourself, with a suggestion for a partner-driven story experience. Your students might suggest an appropriate book or write one themselves.

Space

Figure 7-5

Before the pandemic, fire drills were often the only occasion for which each class had a designated spot outside. During COVID, many teachers seized on the idea of a regular space outside for socially distanced read-alouds, nature journals, and other outdoor learning experiences. School settings vary widely, but here are some ways that teachers have created outdoor spaces:

- ► Grabbing carpet or foam squares, student-made *sit-upons* (directions found online), yoga mats, or old towels to sit on and heading for an available blacktop or grassy area may be all you really need to get outside and read a book. Independent reading under the lone oak tree allows for a sensory and literary experience.

- ► Outdoor classrooms: These are spaces designated for learning. Some schools have dedicated areas for sitting on the ground; others have found tree stumps or made benches with logs.

Figure 7-6

Figure 7-7

Figure 7-8
Logs, stumps, and cable tables can shape a simple outdoor classroom.

Figure 7-9
Paint a wall or boulder with chalkboard paint to provide an outdoor slate.

- ▶ Materials: Students might bring bins, totes, or backpacks of supplies outside for each session, or materials might be shared in a large tub or shed.

- ▶ As the outdoor learning space becomes more popular, you'll have the happy task of creating a physical sign-up sheet in a communal spot or posting an accessible digital one—to accommodate everyone and avoid disappointment.

- ▶ Create other outdoor areas for literacy learning, such as sensory paths, a trail through any woods, a permanent structure for story hikes, and a word garden.

Colleagues

Figure 7-10

Whenever I land a job in a new setting, I always look for that one person who seems to share my goals. You may be lucky to already have this person, and that's all you need to get going. Working with others provides you with a chance to brainstorm, give each other feedback, and discuss successes and ways to tweak your approach. You can also share materials and take turns setting things up. Where might you find these kindred spirits?

- ▶ Professional learning community: Your school might be organized around grade-level teams or PLCs. Describe your outdoor literacy ideas and see what resonates.

- ▶ Specialists: Art, music, physical education, media center/library teachers might be the ones to partner with.

- ► Cross-grade partnerships: If your school has book buddies between grade levels or other student partnerships, you might introduce some outdoor literacy experiences to your classes. One might set up a sensory path or scavenger hunt for another. Older students might create book recommendation paths or StoryWalks® for younger ones.

Volunteers

Figure 7-11

There may be volunteers who would like to get involved, and some of them may even be more comfortable being outdoors than in a traditional indoor classroom.

- ► Invite family members to help with read-alouds, trail-going, or building outdoor spaces or StoryWalk® structures.
- ► PTA volunteers or committees might be interested in helping set up permanent structures on trails, word gardens, and other "hardware" for future literacy experiences.
- ► Community groups and local companies may be education minded. Some companies give paid time off for employees to volunteer.
- ► Local colleges may have outreach groups, education departments, and outing clubs. Elementary students particularly enjoy the energy of this age group.

Resources

Figure 7-12

Broda, Herb. 2007. *Schoolyard-Enhanced Learning: Using the Outdoors as an Instructional Tool, K–8*. Portland, ME: Stenhouse. Presents a wealth of ideas for using the schoolyard for learning, as well as the schoolyard as content.

Broda, Herb. 2011. *Moving the Classroom Outdoors: Schoolyard-Enhanced Learning in Action*. Portland, ME: Stenhouse. Provides many examples across the country of schoolyard learning.

Laws, John Muir, and Emilie Lygren. 2020. *How to Teach Nature Journaling: Curiosity, Wonder, Attention*. Berkeley, CA: Heyday Books.

Robertson, Juliet. 2014. *Dirty Teaching: A Beginner's Guide to Learning Outdoors*. Carmarthen, UK: Independent Thinking Press. This gem of a book offers so many ways to get children outside, from convincing reasons to thoughtful logistics.

Sobel, David. 2008. *Childhood and Nature: Design Principles for Educators.* Portland, ME: Stenhouse. A seminal work that provides a framework for designing outdoor learning in nature.

VanDerwater, Amy Ludwig. 2020–2021. A series of nature-writing videos may be found on her YouTube channel, or on her website (www.amyludwigvanderwater.com) under "Writing/Projects." Collaboration with Mamaroneck UFSD and Sheldrake Environmental Center. Amy invites students to observe and write about nature from her camper, Betsy. Highly engaging and instantly doable.

Children's Books Cited

Ali, A. E. 2020. *Our Favorite Day of the Year*. Illustrated by Rahele Jomepour Bell. New York: Salaam Reads/Simon & Schuster Books for Young Readers.

Arbona, Marion. 2020. *Window*. Toronto, ON: Kids Can Press.

Archer, Micha. 2021. *Wonder Walkers*. New York: Nancy Paulsen Books/Penguin Random House LLC.

Arnold, Katya. 2005. *Elephants Can Paint Too!* New York: Atheneum Books for Young Readers.

Ashman, Linda. 2018. *Outside My Window*. Illustrated by Jamey Christoph. Grand Rapids, MI: Eerdmans Books for Young Readers.

Aston, Dianna Hutts. 2007. *A Seed Is Sleepy*. Illustrated by Sylvia Long. San Francisco: Chronicle Books.

———. 2015. *A Rock Is Lively*. Illustrated by Sylvia Long. San Francisco: Chronicle Books.

Babin, Stephanie. 2019. *Touch and Explore Construction*. Illustrated by Benjamin Becue. San Francisco: Twirl Books/Chronicle.

Bac, F. Sehnaz. 2018. *Stone Painting for Kids: Designs to Spark Your Creativity*. Mineola, NY: Dover Publications.

Bang, Molly, and Penny Chisholm. 2014. *Buried Sunlight: How Fossil Fuels Have Changed the Earth*. New York: The Blue Sky Press.

Banks, Kate. 2006. *Max's Words*. Illustrated by Boris Kulikov. New York: Frances Foster Books/Farrar, Straus and Giroux.

Barrett, Judi. 1978. *Cloudy with a Chance of Meatballs*. Illustrated by Ron Barrett. New York: Aladdin Paperbacks.

Baum, L. Frank. 2015. *The Wizard of Oz*. Illustrated by Charles Santore. Kennebunkport, ME: Applesauce Press.

Baylor, Byrd. 1974. *Everybody Needs a Rock*. Illustrated by Peter Parnall. New York: Atheneum Books for Young Readers.

Beach, Judi K. 2003. *Names for Snow*. Illustrated by Loretta Krupinski. New York: Hyperion Books for Children.

Becker, Aaron. 2013. *Journey*. Book 1 of Aaron Becker's Wordless Trilogy. Somerville, MA: Candlewick Press.

Bodach, Vijaya Khisty. 2018. *Leaves*. Revised ed. North Mankato, MN: Capstone Press.

Boss, Shira. 2018. *Up in the Leaves: The True Story of the Central Park Treehouses*. Illustrated by Jamey Christoph. New York: Union Square Kids.

Brisson, Pat. 1994. *Wanda's Roses*. Illustrated by Maryann Cocca-Leffler. Honesdale, PA: Boyds Mills Press.

———. 2018. *Before We Eat: From Farm to Table*. Illustrated by Mary Azarian. Second ed. Thomaston, ME: Tilbury House.

Bryant, Jen. 2008. *A River of Words: The Story of William Carlos Williams*. Illustrated by Melissa Sweet. Grand Rapids, MI: Eerdmans Books for Young Readers.

———. 2014. *The Right Word: Roget and His Thesaurus*. Illustrated by Melissa Sweet. Grand Rapids, MI: Eerdmans Books for Young Readers.

Bunting, Eve. 1994. *Flower Garden*. Illustrated by Kathryn Hewitt. New York: Harcourt Children's Books.

Burleigh, Robert. 2020. *Tiny Bird: A Hummingbird's Amazing Journey*. Illustrated by Wendell Minor. New York: Henry Holt.

Butterfield, Moira. 2016. *City Trails: New York*. Oakland, CA: Lonely Planet Publications.

———. 2020. *The Secret Life of Trees: Explore the Forests of the World with Oakheart the Brave*. Illustrated by Vivian Mineker. London, UK: Words & Pictures.

Camper, Cathy. 2021. *Ten Ways to Hear Snow*. Illustrated by Kenard Pak. New York: Kokila/ Penguin Random House.

Carle, Eric. 2009. *The Very Hungry Caterpillar*. New York: Philomel Books.

Carlton, Dustin Lee. 2017. *We Love Reading Street Signs*. New York: Confetti Parade House.

———. 2020. *New York City Street Signs: Learn to Read with Environmental Print*. New York: Confetti Parade House.

Cascade Interpretive Consulting. 2004. *Interpretive and Wayfinding Plan: Washington Park Arboretum*. Seattle: Lehrman Cameron Studio.

Cassino, Mark, photographer, with Jon Nelson. 2009. *The Story of Snow: The Science of Winter's Wonder*. San Francisco: Chronicle Books.

Christelow, Eileen. 2018. *Vote!* New York: Clarion Books.

Christian, Peggy. 2008. *If You Find a Rock*. Photographs by Barbara Hirsch Lember. New York: Clarion Books.

Clark, M. H. 2018. *Tiny, Perfect Things*. Illustrated by Madeline Kloepper. Everett, WA: Compendium.

Clark-Robinson, Monica. 2018. *Let the Children March*. Illustrated by Frank Morrison. New York: Clarion Books.

Cordell, Matthew. 2017. *Wolf in the Snow*. New York: Feiwel & Friends/Macmillan.

Cronin, Doreen. 2000. *Click, Clack, Moo: Cows That Type*. Illustrated by Betsy Lewin. New York: Simon & Schuster Children's Publishing.

David, M. Kaye. 2021. *Dirt Machines: Heavy-Duty Construction Vehicles.* Independently published/Amazon Steam Bookworks.

Davies, Nicola. 2012. *Outside Your Window: A First Book of Nature*. Illustrated by Mark Hearld. Somerville, MA: Candlewick Press.

———. 2014. *Tiny Creatures: The World of Microbes*. Illustrated by Emily Sutton. Somerville, MA: Candlewick Press.

———. 2020. *Hummingbird*. Illustrated by Jane Ray. Somerville, MA: Candlewick Press.

Daywalt, Drew. 2013. *The Day the Crayons Quit*. Illustrated by Oliver Jeffers. New York: Philomel Books.

de la Peña, Matt. 2015. *Last Stop on Market Street*. Illustrated by Christian Robinson. New York: G. P. Putnam's Sons for Young Readers.

Delano, Marfe. 2015. *Explore My World Clouds.* Washington, DC: National Geographic Kids.

Denos, Julia, and E. B. Goodale. 2017. *Windows*. Somerville, MA: Candlewick Press.

dePaola, Tomie. 2017. *Strega Nona*. New York: Little Simon.

DiSalvo-Ryan, DyAnne. 1994. *City Green*. New York: Scholastic.

Ehlert, Lois. 1987. *Growing Vegetable Soup*. New York: HMH Books for Young Readers.

———. 1988. *Planting a Rainbow*. New York: HMH Books for Young Readers.

———. 1991. *Red Leaf, Yellow Leaf*. New York: HMH Books for Young Readers.

———. 2005. *Leaf Man*. New York: Harcourt.

Everett, Macaire. 2021. *The World from Our Driveway*. Macairesmuse LLC (self-published).

Farrell, Alison. 2019. *The Hike*. San Francisco: Chronicle Books.

Ferry, Beth. 2021. *Stick and Stone: Best Friends Forever!* Illustrated by Tom Lichtenheld. New York: Clarion Books.

Fine, Edith Hope, and Angela D. Halpin. 2010. *Water, Weed, and Wait*. Illustrated by Colleen M. Madden. Toronto: Tricycle Press/Penguin Random House Canada.

Fleming, Candace. 2020. *Honeybee: The Busy Life of Apis Mellifera*. Illustrated by Eric Rohmann. Toronto: Neal Porter Books/Penguin Random House Canada.

Fleming, Denise. 2006. *Alphabet Under Construction*. New York: Square Fish Books.

———. 2011. *Shout! Shout It Out!* New York: Henry Holt.

Fuhr, Ute, and Raoul Sautai. 2017. *Bees*. UK: Moonlighting Publishing.

Galbraith, Kathryn O. 2011. *Planting the Wild Garden*. Illustrated by Wendy Anderson Halperin. Atlanta: Peachtree Publishers.

Gerber, Carole. 2013. *Seeds, Bees, Butterflies, and More! Poems for Two Voices*. Illustrated by Eugene Yelchin. New York: Henry Holt and Co.

Gibbons, Gail. 2000. *The Honey Makers*. New York: HarperCollins.

———. 2004. *Tell Me, Tree: All About Trees for Kids*. New York: Scholastic.

Gladstone, James. 2019. *My Winter City*. Illustrated by Gary Clement. Toronto: Groundwood Books/House of Anansi Press.

Gómez, Bianca. 2021. *Bird House*. New York: Abrams Books.

Gomi, Tarō. 2001. *Everyone Poops*. Translated by Amanda Mayer Stinchecum. San Diego: Kane/Miller Books.

Graf, Mike. 2021. *My Awesome Field Guide to North American Birds: Find and Identify Your Feathered Friends*. New York: Rockridge Press.

Graham, Joan Bransfield. 1994. *Splish Splash*. Illustrated by Steven Scott. New York: Houghton Mifflin.

———. 1999. *Flicker Flash*. Illustrated by Nancy Davis. New York: Houghton Mifflin.

Guest, Patrick. 2020. *Windows*. Illustrated by Jonathan Bentley. Richmond: Hardie Grant Publishing.

Guillain, Charlotte. 2017. *The Street Beneath My Feet*. Illustrated by Yuval Zommer. London: Quarto Publishing.

Hale, Christy. 2020. *Out the Door*. New York: Holiday House.

Harris, Shawn. 2021. *Have You Ever Seen a Flower?* San Francisco: Chronicle Books.

Hegarty, Patricia. 2017. *Bee: Nature's Tiny Miracle*. Illustrated by Britta Teckentrup. New York: Doubleday.

Heos, Bridget. 2013. *Let's Meet a Construction Worker*. Illustrated by Mike Moran. Minneapolis, MN: Lerner Digital Publishing.

Hibbs, Gillian. 2018. *Errol's Garden*. Swindon, UK: Child's Play International, Ltd.

High, Linda Oatman. 2002. *Beekeepers*. Illustrated by Doug Chayka. New York: Boyds Mills Press.

Hines, Anne Grossnickle. 2005. *Winter Lights: A Season in Poems & Quilts*. New York: HarperCollins.

Hoban, Tana. 1983. *I Read Signs*. New York: HarperCollins.

———. 1999. *I Read Symbols*. New York: HarperCollins.

Hodgson, Rob. 2021. *When Cloud Became a Cloud*. London: Penguin Young Readers.

Holub, Joan. 2013. *Little Red Writing*. Illustrated by Melissa Sweet. San Francisco: Chronicle Books.

———. 2020. *Runaway Signs*. Illustrated by Allison Farrell. London: Penguin Young Readers.

Hopkins, H. Joseph. 2013. *The Tree Lady: The True Story of How One Tree-Loving Woman Changed a City Forever*. Illustrated by Jill McElmurry. San Diego: Beach Lane Books.

Hopkins, Lee Bennett, ed. 2010. *Sharing the Seasons: A Book of Poems*. Illustrated by David Diaz. New York: Margaret K. McElderberry Books.

———. 2020. *Construction People*. Illustrated by Ellen Shi. New York: Astra Publishing House.

Jaco Design. 2020. *I Spy with My Little Eye: Construction Vehicles*. Seattle: Amazon Digital Services, LLC.

Janeczko, Paul B. 2001. *A Poke in the I: A Collection of Concrete Poems*. Illustrated by Chris Raschka. Somerville, MA: Candlewick Press.

Jenkins, Emily. 2012. *Lemonade in Winter: A Book About Two Kids Counting Money*. Illustrated by G. Brian Karas. Toronto: Schwartz & Wade Books.

Jenkins, Steve. 2004. *Actual Size*. New York: Houghton Mifflin.

Jenkins, Steve, and Robin Page. 2003. *What Do You Do with a Tail Like This?* New York: Houghton Mifflin.

———. 2015. *How to Swallow a Pig: Step-by-Step Advice from the Animal Kingdom*. New York: Houghton Mifflin Harcourt.

Johnston, Tony. 2021. *Trees*. Illustrated by Tiffany Bozic. New York: Simon & Schuster/ Paula Wiseman Books.

Judge, Lita. 2021. *The Wisdom of Trees: How Trees Work Together to Form a Natural Kingdom*. New York: Roaring Brook Press.

Juster, Norton. 2005. *The Hello, Goodbye Window*. Illustrated by Chris Raschka. New York: Michael diCapua Books/Hyperion Books for Children.

Keating, Jess. 2016. *Pink Is for Blobfish: Discovering the World's Perfectly Pink Animals*. Illustrated by David DeGrand. New York: Alfred A. Knopf.

Keats, Ezra Jack. 1962. *The Snowy Day*. New York: Viking Press.

Kelley, Gerald. 2021. *Please Please the Bees*. Park Ridge, IL: Albert Whitman.

Ketchum, Liza., Jaqueline Briggs Martin, and Phyllis Root. 2021. *Begin with a Bee*. Illustrated by Claudia McGehee. Minneapolis, MN: University of Minnesota Press.

Khan, Rukhsana. 2010. *Big Red Lollipop*. Illustrated by Sophie Blackall. New York: Penguin Young Readers Group.

Kiesler, Kate. 2002. *Wings on the Wind: Bird Poems*. New York: Clarion Books.

King, Nancy. 2018. *Stop, Wait, Go! Road Signs and Symbols It's Fun to Know!* Scotts Valley, CA: CreateSpace Independent Publishing Platform.

Klassen, Jon. 2021. *The Rock from the Sky*. Somerville, MA: Candlewick Press.

Kooser, Ted, and Connie Wanek. 2022. *Marshmallow Clouds: Two Poets at Play Among Figures of Speech*. Illustrated by Richard Jones. Somerville, MA: Candlewick Press.

Krebs, Laurie. 2020. *The Beeman*. Illustrated by Valerie Cis. Concord, MA: Barefoot Books.

Laminack, Lester. 2007. *Snow Day!* Illustrated by Adam Gustavson. Atlanta: Peachtree Publishers.

Lark, Rainbow. 2020. *I Spy with My Little Eye: Construction Site*. Independently published.

Larkin, Shabazz. 2019. *The Thing About Bees: A Love Letter*. San Francisco: Readers to Eaters Press.

Laws, John Muir, and Emilie Lygren. 2020. *How to Teach Nature Journaling: Curiosity, Wonder, Attention*. Berkeley, CA: Heyday Books.

Lawson, JonArno. 2016. *Sidewalk Flowers*. Illustrated by Sydney Smith. Toronto: Groundwood Books/House of Anansi Press.

Lebeuf, Darren. 2019. *My Forest Is Green*. Illustrated by Ashley Barron. Toronto: Kids Can Press.

Ledyard, Stephanie Parsley. 2018. *Pie Is for Sharing*. Illustrated by Jason Chin. New York: Roaring Brook Press.

Lesser, Rika. 1999. *Hansel and Gretel*. Illustrated by Paul O. Zelinsky. New York: Puffin Press.

Lloyd, Megan Wagner. 2016. *Finding Wild*. Illustrated by Abigail Halpin. New York: Alfred A. Knopf.

Lyons, Shelly. 2013. *Signs in My Neighborhood*. Mankato, MN: Capstone Press.

Macken, Joann Early. 2016. *Flip, Float, Fly: Seeds on the Move*. Illustrated by Pam Paparone. New York: Holiday House Press.

Maestro, Betsy. 1994. *Why Do Leaves Change Color?* Illustrated by Loretta Krupinski. New York: HarperCollins.

Maret, Sherri. 2017. *The Cloud Artist: A Choctaw Tale*. Translated by Dora Wickson. Illustrated by Merisha Sequoia Clark. Oklahoma City, OK: RoadRunner Press.

Markel, Michelle. 2013. *Brave Girl: Clara and the Shirtwaist Makers' Strike of 1909*. Illustrated by Melissa Sweet. New York: Balzer + Bray/ HarperCollins.

Martin, Jacqueline Briggs. 1998. *Snowflake Bentley*. Illustrated by Mary Azarian. New York: Houghton Mifflin.

Martinez-Neal, Juana. 2018. *Alma and How She Got Her Name*. Somerville, MA: Candlewick Press.

McCully, Emily Arnold. 1996. *The Bobbin Girl*. New York: Dial Books for Young Readers.

McLerran, Alice. 1991. *Roxaboxen*. Illustrated by Barbara Cooney. New York: HarperCollins.

Medina, Meg. 2018. *Merci Suárez Changes Gears*. Somerville, MA: Candlewick Press.

Messner, Kate. 2011. *Over and Under the Snow*. Illustrated by Christopher Silas Neal. San Francisco: Chronicle Books.

———. 2015. *Up in the Garden and Down in the Dirt*. Illustrated by Christopher Silas Neal. San Francisco: Chronicle Books.

Miller, Pat Zietlow. 2021. *What Can You Do with a Rock?* Illustrated by Katie Kath. Naperville, IL: Sourcebooks, Inc.

Montgomery, Heather L. 2021. *What's in Your Pocket? Collecting Nature's Treasures*. Illustrated by Maribel Lechuga. Watertown, MA: Charlesbridge Publishing.

Mora, Oge. 2019. *Saturday*. New York: Little, Brown Books for Young Readers.

Morrison, Gordon. 2004. *Nature in the Neighborhood*. New York: Houghton Mifflin.

Mullen, Diane C. 2020. *One Little Lot: The 1-2-3s of an Urban Garden*. Illustrated by Oriol Vidal. Watertown, MA: Charlesbridge Publishing.

Oxlade, Chris. 2018. *Construction Machines*. Richmond Hill, ON: Firefly Books.

Pak, Kenard. 2016. *Goodbye Summer, Hello Autumn*. New York: Henry Holt and Company.

———. 2017. *Goodbye Autumn, Hello Winter*. New York: Henry Holt and Company.

———. 2020. *Goodbye Winter, Hello Spring*. New York: Henry Holt and Company.

Pallotta, Jerry. 2006. *The Construction Alphabet Book*. Illustrated by Rob Bolster. Watertown, MA: Charlesbridge Publishing.

Paschkis, Julie. 2021. *The Wordy Book*. Brooklyn, NY: Enchanted Lion Books.

Perkins, Lynne Rae. 2003. *Snow Music*. New York: Greenwillow Books/HarperCollins.

Pollak, Barbara. 2004. *Our Community Garden*. New York: Alladin/Beyond Words/Simon & Schuster.

Pollock, Penny. 2001. *When the Moon Is Full: A Lunar Year*. Illustrated by Mary Azarian. New York: Little, Brown.

Posada, Mia. 2000. *Dandelions: Stars in the Grass*. Minneapolis, MN: Carolrhoda Books.

Preus, Margi. 2016. *Celebritrees: Historic & Famous Trees of the World*. Illustrated by Rebecca Gibbon. New York: Henry Holt and Company.

Pryor, Katherine. 2019. *Bea's Bees*. Illustrated by Ellie Peterson. Atglen, PA: Schiffer Publishing.

Ralston, Fraser, and Judith Ralston. 2021. *What's the Weather? Clouds, Climate, and Global Warming*. New York: Dorling Kindersley Publishing.

Rau, Dana Meachen. 2006. *Fluffy, Flat, and Wet: A Book About Clouds*. Illustrated by Denise Shea. Minneapolis: Picture Window Books.

Reynolds, Peter H. 2018. *The Word Collector*. New York: Scholastic.

Rinker, Sherri Duskey. 2011. *Goodnight, Goodnight, Construction Site*. Illustrated by Tom Lichtenheld. San Francisco: Chronicle Books.

———. 2020. *Construction Site Mission: Demolition!* Illustrated by AG Ford. San Francisco: Chronicle Books.

Rivers, Kristine. 2021. *Exploring Birds Activity Book for Kids: 50 Creative Projects to Inspire Curiosity & Discovery*. New York: Rockridge Press.

Roberts, Bethany. 2001. *The Wind's Garden*. Illustrated by Melanie Hope Greenberg. New York: Henry Holt.

Rockwell, Anne. 2008. *Clouds.* Illustrated by Frané Lessac. New York: HarperCollins.

Rogers, Lisa. 2019. *16 Words: William Carlos Williams and "The Red Wheelbarrow."* Illustrated by Chuck Groenink. New York: Random House Children's Books.

Rosenstock, Barb. 2018. *Through the Window: Views of Marc Chagall's Life and Art*. Illustrated by Mary GrandPre. New York: Random House Children's Books.

Samoyault, Tiphaine. 1997. *Give Me a Sign! What Pictograms Tell Us Without Words*. New York: Viking.

Schaefer, Lola M., and Adam Schaefer. 2016. *Because of an Acorn*. Illustrated by Frann Preston-Gannon. San Francisco: Chronicle Books.

Schaub, Michelle. 2017. *Fresh-Picked Poetry: A Day at the Farmers' Market*. Illustrated by Amy Huntington. Watertown, MA: Charlesbridge Publishing.

Schotter, Roni. 2013. *The Boy Who Loved Words*. Illustrated by Giselle Potter. New York: Random House Children's Books.

Schulman, Janet. 2008. *Pale Male: Citizen Hawk of New York City*. Illustrated by Meilo So. New York: Alfred A. Knopf.

Scott, Jordan. 2020. *I Talk Like a River*. Illustrated by Sydney Smith. New York: Holiday House.

Seuss, Dr. [Theodor Geisel]. 2012. *The Lorax*. New York: HarperCollins.

Shannon, David. 1998. *A Bad Case of Stripes*. New York: Blue Sky Press/HarperCollins.

Shaw, Charles G. 1988. *It Looked Like Spilt Milk*. New York: HarperCollins.

Sidman, Joyce. 2006. *Meow Ruff*. Illustrated by Michelle Berg. New York: Houghton Mifflin.

———. 2011. *Swirl by Swirl: Spirals in Nature*. Illustrated by Beth Krommes. New York: Houghton Mifflin Harcourt.

Silver, Donald. 1993. *One Small Square: Backyard*. Illustrated by Patricia Wynne. New York: McGraw-Hill.

———. 1995. *One Small Square: Woods.* Illustrated by Patricia Wynne. New York: McGraw-Hill.

Silverstein, Shel. 2004. *Where the Sidewalk Ends: The Poems & Drawings of Shel Silverstein*. New York: HarperCollins.

Singer, Marilyn. 2012. *A Stick Is an Excellent Thing: Poems Celebrating Outdoor Play*. Illustrated by LeUyen Pham. New York: HarperCollins.

Smith, Sydney. 2019. *Small in the City*. Toronto: Groundwood Books/House of Anansi Press.

Sondheim, Stephen, et al. 1999. *Into the Woods*. Chatsworth, CA: Distributed by Image Entertainment.

Soontornvat, Christina. 2020. *All Thirteen: The Incredible Cave Rescue of the Thai Boys' Soccer Team*. Somerville, MA: Candlewick Press.

Stemple, Heidi E.Y. 2018. *Counting Birds: The Idea That Helped Save Our Feathered Friends*. Illustrated by Clover Robin. Lake Forest, CA: Seagrass Press/Quarto.

Stewart, Melissa. 2011. *A Place for Butterflies*. Illustrated by Higgins Bond. Atlanta, GA: Peachtree Publishers.

———. 2017. *Can an Aardvark Bark?* Illustrated by Steve Jenkins. San Diego: Beach Lane Books.

Stewart, Melissa, and Allen Young. 2013. *No Monkeys, No Chocolate*. Illustrated by Nicole Wong. Watertown, MA: Charlesbridge Publishing.

Stewart, Sarah. 1997. *The Gardener*. Illustrated by David Small. New York: Farrar, Strauss and Giroux.

Stier, Catherine. 2007. *If I Ran for President*. Illustrated by Lynne Avril. Park Ridge, IL: Albert Whitman & Co.

Stockdale, Susan. 2020. *Bring on the Birds*. Atlanta, GA: Peachtree Press.

Sullivan, Martha. 2015. *If You Love Honey: Nature's Connections*. Illustrated by Cathy Morrison. Nevada City, CA: Dawn Publications.

Talbott, Hudson. 2021. *A Walk in the Words*. New York: Penguin Young Readers Group.

Trusiani, Lisa. 2021. *All About Rocks and Minerals: An Introduction for Kids*. New York: Callisto Media.

Udry, Janice May. 1987. *A Tree Is Nice*. Illustrated by Marc Simont. New York: HarperTrophy.

Van Slyke, Rebecca. 2017. *Lexie the Word Wrangler*. Illustrated by Jessie Hartland. New York: Nancy Paulsen Books/Penguin Random House.

VanDerwater, Amy Ludwig. 2013. *Forest Has a Song: Poems*. Illustrated by Robin Gourley. New York: Clarion Books.

———. 2016. *Every Day Birds*. Illustrated by Dylan Metrano. New York: Scholastic.

Verde, Susan, and Georgie Badiel. 2018. *The Water Princess*. Illustrated by Peter H. Reynolds. New York: G. P. Putnam's Sons.

Wallace, Mary. 2004. *Make Your Own Inuksuk*. Toronto: Owlkids Books.

Ward, Jennifer. 2014. *Mama Built a Little Nest*. Illustrated by Steve Jenkins. San Diego: Beach Lane Books.

———. 2020. *How to Find a Bird*. Illustrated by Diana Sudyka. San Diego: Beach Lane Books.

Watts, Mar Theilgaard. 1991. *Tree Finder: A Manual for the Identification of Trees by Their Leaves*. Rochester, NY: Nature Study Guild.

Watts, Mar Theilgaard, and Tom Watts. 1970. *Winter Tree Finder: A Manual for Identifying Deciduous Trees in Winter*. Rochester, NY: Nature Study Guild.

Weekes, Russell. 2015. *A Book About Signs*. London: Cicada Books.

Wenzel, Brendan. 2019. *A Stone Sat Still*. San Francisco: Chronicle Books.

Wheeler, Eliza. 2019. *Home in the Woods*. New York: Nancy Paulsen Books/Penguin.

White, E. B. 1952. *Charlotte's Web*. Illustrated by Garth Williams. New York: Harper & Row.

Winter, Jeanette. 2019. *Our House Is on Fire: Greta Thunberg's Call to Save the Planet*. San Diego: Beach Lane Books.

Woodson, Jacqueline. 2018. *The Day You Begin*. Illustrated by Rafael López. New York: Nancy Paulsen Books/Penguin.

Yang, Kelly. 2018. *Front Desk*. New York: Arthur A. Levine Books/Scholastic.

Yolen, Jane. 2020. *Knowing the Name of a Bird*. Illustrated by Jori van der Linde. Mankato, MN: The Creative Company.

Professional Resources Cited

Broda, Herbert W. 2007. *Schoolyard-Enhanced Learning: Using the Outdoors as an Instructional Tool, K–8*. Portland, ME: Stenhouse.

———. 2011. *Moving the Classroom Outdoors: Schoolyard-Enhanced Learning in Action*. Portland, ME: Stenhouse.

Caputo, Paul, Shea Lewis, and Lisa Brochu. 2008. *Interpretation by Design: Graphic Design Basics for Heritage Interpreters*. National Association for Interpretation (NAI). Fort Collins, CO: InterpPress.

Centre for Excellence in Universal Design. "What is Universal Design?" (website division). Accessed August 9, 2022. National Disability Authority (NDA). http://www.universaldesign.ie.

Curious City: Children's Book Engagement Tools (website). Accessed August 10, 2022. http://www.curiouscitydpw.com/storywalk.

Gross, Michael, Ronald Zimmerman, and Jim Buchholz. 2006. *Signs, Trails, and Wayside Exhibits: Connecting People and Places*. 3rd ed. Stevens Point, WI: University of Wisconsin-Stevens Point Foundation Press.

Heard, Georgia. 1999. *Awakening the Heart: Exploring Poetry in Elementary and Middle School*. Portsmouth, NH: Heinemann.

Kellogg-Hubbard Library. "StoryWalk®." https://www.kellogghubbard.org/storywalk. Created by Anne Ferguson, Montpelier, VT.

Laws, John Muir. John Muir Laws: Nature Stewardship Through Science, Education, and Art (website.) Accessed August 9, 2022. http://johnmuirlaws.com.

Louv, Richard. 2008. *Last Child in the Woods: Saving our Children from Nature-Deficit Disorder*. Chapel Hill, NC: Algonquin Books of Chapel Hill.

McGregor, Tanny. 2018. *Ink & Ideas: Sketchnotes for Engagement, Comprehension, and Thinking*. Portsmouth, NH: Heinemann.

Mobile Museum Project. 2019. *Curating a School Museum: Teachers' Handbook*. London: Royal Holloway, University of London and Royal Botanic Gardens, Kew.

Moline, Steve. 1995. *I See What You Mean: Children at Work with Visual Information*. Portland, ME: Stenhouse.

———. 2011. *I See What You Mean: Visual Literacy K–8*. 2nd ed. Portland, ME: Stenhouse.

Pearson, P. David., and Margaret C. Gallagher. 1983. *The Instruction of Reading Comprehension*. Technical Report no. 297. Center for the Study of Reading. Urbana, IL: University of Illinois; Cambridge, MA: Bolt, Beranek, and Newman, Inc.; and Washington, DC: National Institute of Education.

Robertson, Juliet. 2014. *Dirty Teaching: A Beginner's Guide to Learning Outdoors.* Carmarthen, Wales, UK: Independent Thinking Press.

Sobel, David. 2008. *Childhood and Nature: Design Principles for Educators*. Portland, ME: Stenhouse.

Tilden, Freeman. 2013. *Interpreting Our Heritage.* Durham, NC: The University of North Carolina Press.

VanDerwater, Amy Ludwig. 2018. *Poems Are Teachers: How Studying Poetry Strengthens Writing in All Genres*. Portsmouth, NH: Heinemann.